Waking Up on the Camino

all i know so far

Sabrie King

Copyright © 2024 by Sabrie King

All rights reserved.

No portion of this book may be reproduced, in whole or in part, in any form (except for brief passages quoted in a review), without prior written permission from the author, as permitted by U.S. copyright law.

The lines of *The Prayer of La Faba* are a gift to pilgrims passing through O Cebreiro who visit Santuario de Santa María a Real do Cebreiro and are available to anyone for free online and in print.

Alexander John Shaia kindly granted the author quotes from his book, *Returning From Camino*, to explain significant moments one might experience along a spiritual journey and/or rite of passage.

Camino map source: *The French Way of the Camino de Santiago*, digital image, Responsible Travel, accessed December 2023, <https://www.responsibletravel.com/holidays/camino-de-santiago/travel-guide/the-french-way>

Elevation map source: *Elevation Profile*, digital image, Pilgrim, accessed December 2023, <https://www.pilgrim.es/en/french-way/>

Cover art: *The Collector* ©2019 Elisabeth Ladwig | elisabethonearth.com

Cover design: Robin Locke Monda

Many of the names of the people in this book have been changed to respect their right to privacy. The people and their stories are real, however, and are told within this book with the utmost care and to the best of the author's recollection.

for Dad,
it'll all work out are words of yours
that hold a permanent place in my heart.
thank you. i love you.

for Kym,
soul sisters forever dancing.
this one's for us both.
always & forever (forever & always)

and for my kids,
Addison, Elizabeth, and Finn,
you are the ground that keeps me steady
and the wind that lifts me to fly.
to the moon and to Saturn and back,
i love you.

Camino Francés, or The French Way

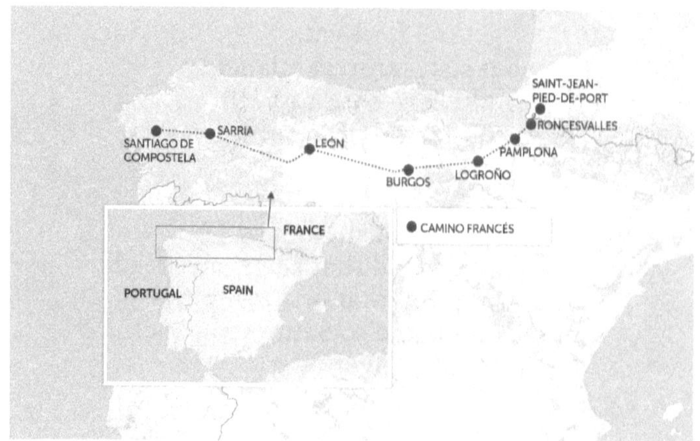

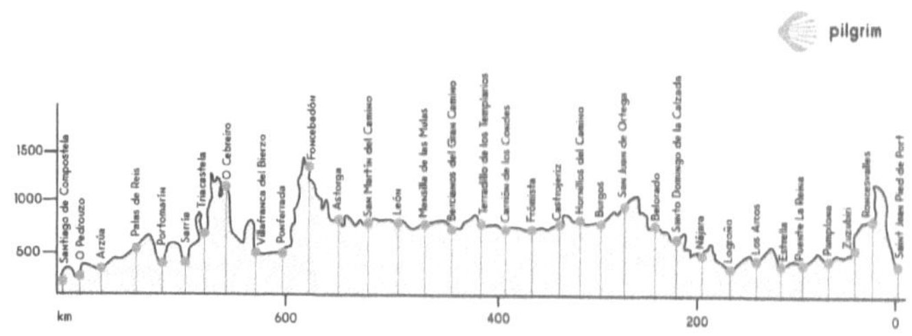

contents

the breakdown and the call

"The loneliest moment in someone's life
is when they are watching their whole world fall apart
and all they can do is stare blankly."

- F. Scott Fitzgerald

journal entry: September 3, 2021

i signed the papers
for the sale of the house today.
Feels strange.

That house
i thought we'd be in until
the kids were older and out on their own.
That house
we'd continue our lives together,
working through troubles
and trials,
happiness and tears.
(Isn't that what it's all about?
The ebbs, the flows,
the softness, the rocky edges,
the fights, the make-ups,
the compromises, the celebrations...)
That house
i thought we'd sell together
and look for another to continue our lives
as empty-nesters, as a growing couple getting older.
That house -

it once was.

Once a place of laughter and plans.
Once a place of dreams and desires.
Once a soft place to fall and land.
But all at once, no longer is it all that.
No,
no longer is it any of that.
It's selling.
Under contract.
Like my life at this very moment,
under the pen strokes of another hand
short, not so sweet,
indecipherable legal jargon meant to confuse and bewilder.
Teased and tormented

turned into something else at the hammer's hit.
Give in and let another take over.
Surrender.
i don't feel strong enough to fight it.
Should i fight it? ... i've fought for so long.
i fought for you, i fought for me,
i fought to give you what you wanted
but it wasn't enough.
Am i enough? Am i too much?
This, you have me wondering.
But maybe this is what i should be wondering...
This life. Its destruction.
This forced hand to let go
of the past, of the present,
of a future that will never be.
This hurt, this disappointment,
this pain that triggers every childhood struggle
hitting deep within the corners of my mind
ever so ready to (re)surface when i'm scared,
when i'm lonely,
or feeling insecure,
or questioning myself,
the silent fight within
leftover from my alcoholic home that's
held
me
in
its
grips
and found its way
into each of my marriages,
one way or another.
Ever since
that first hit,
that first scare
behind closed doors,
that girlhood fright of being alone,
of being left alone...
this is the root of all my fears.
All of it,
every single moment of my turbulent childhood

led me here.

But where is here?

i know my past.
i see it (re)playing right before me.
Heal. Learn.
(i know)
but my present, i need to know.
This broken marriage,
this foreboding aloneness (again),
it's happening again,
this people-pleasing state of mind
that's supposed to keep me safe but
makes me sick
over and over again
until, what do i do? Please again,
forget myself, give my all to others,
day in, day out
according to what others think or how others believe
i should be,
avoiding conflict or disruption...
i know it all (re)appears to teach me a lesson,
yes, this i know.
But i don't want to know this anymore.
i don't want to feel these lessons anymore,
i don't want to play these games or
unravel these quilts i've knitted together time and time
again
anymore.
i want to stop them.
Stop sabotaging things.
Stop sabotaging me.

Am i blaming myself
when i should be listening to myself?
i say, this is the space i need to hold.
i am the person i need to hold.
But am i listening?

you didn't see

you didn't see
the hope she pulled together,
thread by thread,
only to have it unravel like an old woolen scarf
that got tumbled in the dryer way too many times.

you didn't see
the life she dreamt with you,
two spirits together as one
at the river's edge that cloudless July night,
because unless it was one that modeled your rules,
you wore blinders day and night, a view only for you.

you didn't see
the promises you sculpted
and the hopes you drew in vivid colors,
all over again
only to rip them apart in front of her dreams
with a smirk and a sneer and a look she'll never forget.

you didn't see her roots
and how thirsty they were.

you didn't see her leaves
and how sunburnt they were.

you didn't see her blossoms
and how starved they were.

you didn't see the demons
she told to be quiet,
or the shadows she so blindingly lit
thinking she was too much for you.
when in the end, she was right...
she was too much for you.
or was she really?
were you too much for her?

all i wanted

all i wanted was to be seen and feel heard.
to be understood.
and in your eyes,
you may have thought you tried
but you really didn't, did you?
only the bare minimum to get by,
to get through the days that had us cramped
in the house
because of pandemic rules and buckets of fear.
was it too much?
was it all too much?
sharing a home. me and the kids. life with teenagers.
the uncertainty of tomorrow.
was it always too much and i just didn't see?

things had to go your way or be talked into
your way,
but things were so much more
than what you chose to see.
like when you didn't believe me
about one of your friends.
you asked specific questions, like
"what were you wearing?"
and wanted specific answers that i couldn't give.
your assuming shame paralyzed my voice.
i was seeking your soul
and all you gave was a void.
i didn't answer as you thought i should,
so i must be in the wrong...
was i wrong though?
all i wanted was to be seen and feel heard.

when she died, you said
"We all knew this would happen."
(f*ck you, man!)
my lifeless limbs fell to the floor
and you didn't catch them.
why didn't you catch them?

why could you not be there for me?
why did you make me have dinner with others
the evening of her memorial when i was
so clearly in pieces?
why could you not understand?
why did you go out
that same night
when i was sodden with tears,
needing someone to be there?
why could you not be there?
all i wanted was to be seen and feel heard.

this was the beginning of the end.
or was it?
was the beginning of the end earlier for you?
did you see the end before me
just to hold on
and drag me further?
did you see the end before my dad died
only to delay the break
'til after his death
for fear of tainting your word to him?
did you see the end before Kym died
knowing she'd kick your ass if you hurt me
again?

maybe you didn't have the capacity to believe.
maybe you didn't have the capacity to try.
maybe you don't have the capacity to love
truly love
unconditionally
without expectations
or hard-driven tests and obstacles to climb.
maybe it was never meant to be,
maybe i'm coming to know this now.
my logical mind says it's not my fault,
it's not my doing.
but you and i both know
i'm led by the heart and intuition,
not logic.
this isn't logical.

i'm trying to thread it all together
but all my threads are tangled.
i am angry. i am hurt.
three strikes, you're out, Jude.
how dare you?
how dare you make me fall in love with you

again.

it's time for me to understand this.
it's time for me to break away
forever
and let you go.
it's time for me to release any responsibility
for the bad behavior of others.
it's time for me to stop believing i'm too emotional
or i'm too much.
because i'm not.
i'm me.

all i wanted was to be seen and feel heard.
that's all i ever wanted.

i hate the night

i hate the night

(but i love the night too -
in a way the stars love the moon,
sitting next to a gorgeously lit
reflective ball
floating in space, admiring its size
but a bit jealous of its confidence
and knowledge.
nights can be beautiful
especially when they're clear and still
but)

nights can be equally awful
because that's when insecurities come out and
feel real.

as a child,
the night was what brought all the bad things.
growing up in an alcoholic home
with my father disappearing into the bottle
and my mother... well, more
worried about shaming him
than exploring that within her
that made her feel inadequate and unworthy still.

my nights were as turbulent
as a hurricane coming in from the south.
sure she was doing what she thought was best,
my mother,
she loved us,
i know this and always have,
and my father did too.
i know my father weathered vicious storms
in his mind,
but you don't know this as a child.
all i knew was my night
crashing to the floor.

all I knew was that i couldn't rely on anyone
in my house for comfort,
arms to crawl into and understand me,
hands to wipe the tears away and reassure i'm safe,
a heart to piece back my brokenness with
gold and tape.
i never knew when my night would break down.
i never knew when i'd be on my own
in the dark,
in the corner as the monsters came out
from underneath the bed,
no one to hold my space or guide me to
a soft place to fall.
i never knew when the sky would crack
and lose its shine,
for the night was scary
and held so many sharp corners
ready to pierce right through.

this blindfolded childhood
is what i knew.
it's what kept me going,
when i was all alone.
day to night. night to day,
finding my way through a dark maze with
no moon to light the night's sky.

it happened more often
than any child should have to count.
the fights.
the arguing.
the hits.
the scares.
the fear to bring anyone in
for they'd surely discover my truth.

but this is what i knew,
and not knowing any different,
this is where i learned love to be.
and so i looked for it and
(re)created it in my first marriage,

then my second...

found men who were not and could not
provide a safe place for me to unfold.
i know this now.

this is me. this is who i am.

but these patterns aren't me
and i need to move on. but damn...
living with this fear of rejection,
the memories of crying in a dark room alone
hit deep within these scars still open.
i feel inadequate.
i feel unworthy.
i feel unlovable.
i feel "too much"
and it seeps into every relationship
i've ever had
from then to now.

there's no denying them -
my fears, my insecurities,
for they come at the darkest of times
in the darkest of nights,
and this is why i hate the night,
my wounds find the dark sky above and
seek guidance from those
deceptive balls of fire,
only to find a suffocation that holds
no life at all.

i need to breathe air
into my nights.
i need to hold my fears
in a place
where all that i am falls soundly asleep
because i do love the night,
as weird as it may seem.
my fears and i just walk
a narrowly guided

slippery balance beam,
crying to feel heard and be seen.

at the turn of midnight's watch

because at the turn of midnight's watch
i still remember how it was,
all alone,
how i crumbled
like a pie crust on a cold kitchen floor,
how i faded into the dark
like a candle at its wick's end.
god, how it all remains
so deep and dark within,
how i remember all too well.
i don't know if i can forgive
(i will never forget)
but i can find peace
and know
you will never be allowed near my heart.
no, not ever again.

"One does not choose
to walk the Camino de Santiago...
the Camino chooses the pilgrim."

- Silvio Sirias

journal entry: September 16, 2021

i had a dream last night
a vivid dream
that i had a baby.
She was soft and round,
with a sweet face
and felt like home.
Her name was Sabrie
and her cries were eased
only by my touch.
Other people tried
to calm her nerves
but had no success.
She cried and cried
and cried until
i picked her up.
She looked at me
with soft green eyes
and settled instantly,
into my neck and shoulders,
she melted and
found peace.

that familiar feeling

there's a familiar feeling when
the seasons begin to change...
it's like you're watching the end of a movie
memorized by heart,
the rain...

falls and the autumn leaves turn,
the sun threatens to leave,
no longer does it burn.

the last flower blooms then
fades with the summer sky,
you wonder if you'll ever see color again
to paint your daydreams,
you wonder why...

will you make it through winter
without your limbs falling to frostbite?
will you find warmth along your path,
this gray-ing of days in the dying of light?

but just as the sun
peeks through to provide warmth
to a frigid and frozen world,
love looks in and reminds you
to pick up your heart,
to restore your faith and
build your smile again.
in this, my dear,
you've got a new friend.

at any time, another freeze
could come and break your bones,
this you know all too well
from your life's undertones.
but warm from the winter sun,
you walk the melting landscape
trusting you'll know what to do

the next time
the ice breaks.

in a café

i was sitting in a café.
empty tables and empty chairs.
only mine was occupied
and that was completely fine.

i was working on my novel.
finishing my novel, to be exact -
for on that day,
my novel concluded itself.
it wrote its ending to itself
and urged me to move on.

but on to what?

i sat there,
having written the end to these pages
that got me through
my dad's death,
my best friend's death,
my marriage's death,
all in a matter of months.

but now what?

i needed something,
this first-draft,
this get-the-story-out-and-onto-paper version
was complete,
this entity that pulled me from
each moment to the next.
every. single. day.
for the last nine months.

i had nothing to pull me through now.

where was i to go? what was i to do?
what was there to fill my evenings
and silent moments?

there was nothing for me to grab onto.
i felt lost.

(when things are uncertain,
this is what Sabrie does.
she gets scared, pushes people away
and runs.
that's what she learned at a far too young age
and how she made it through the world
around her today.
little Sabrie knows
all too well
what darkness can fall
at any given moment.)

i am a runner.
i know this.
i've always been a runner.
when things get tough,
when i feel the floorboards cracking
and breaking from underneath me,
i run.
physically...
mentally,
i get the hell out of there
because i know what's coming,
a tidal wave or
a mountain crumbling to the dust.

i'm grateful for the ability to run,
for the knowledge in my head,
the strength in my legs,
the lessons in my heart
that fear and running have taught.
when i needed it most, my running was there.
for my safety and security, running was everywhere.

but "do i need to run?" is what i played
over and over in my head, on this day.
the day i was in the café.
the day i finished my novel.

the day i wondered what was next.

i don't know.
was running what i was doing, or
was running what i was
needing to do?
for there was no imminent danger,
no physical threat to my being,
no unsafe place that i retreated to...
but with everything seeming to die around me,
i needed to run,
i needed to let go...

(they say the Camino calls when you're ready,
you're summoned
from out of nowhere)

...i needed somewhere far away,
somewhere that held space enough for me
to turn into someone new.
who that someone was ... i wasn't sure
but that Somewhere was calling my name
and it was calling me
NOW.

its voice began to whisper
through the cracks in my soul,
deep down
and drew me in.

i had lost nearly everything i thought was real.
this was the only spark of hope
left deep in my heart
and it burned bright.

i composed my resignation
from a career of 20 years and planned to leave
my home
my kids
for a total of 50 days
for a place i'd never been to

nor knew anything about,
to embark on a journey
across lands that seemed only tales in books.
i'd never done anything like this before,
walk 800 kilometers/500 miles
through something so foreign to me as my own self.

bring your pieces and burdens and walk with me,
leave everything behind
and meet yourself
on the other side, it said.

the Camino knew... even at this time

i created a playlist to train
for the Camino,
to prep, to pack, to workout to -
added songs that inspire and push me further,
pulled a random photo from the internet
when i searched "photos of the Camino"
and chose one for its beauty, its coastal position
...and its stairs that zigzagged across the ocean.

i didn't know where it was in Spain,
at this time.
nor did i know its name.
i didn't know this place even existed,
at this time,
or that it was a tourist destination.
but somewhere in the secrets of my mind,
my subconscious knew my journey
would come full circle
in this very spot,
at this time.

and even though my survival mind was clueless,
packed and (almost) ready to go...
the Camino knew,
even at this time,
where i'd turn around and head home.

almost go-time

"One cannot discover new oceans
unless he has the courage to lose sight of the shore."

- André Gide

am i running from or running to?

i am leaving.
i am running.
i am quitting my job
and going somewhere far away.
to a place where my name doesn't sound so different.
to where the road ends and the mountains begin.

quitting my career of 20 years
was the scariest,
best decision
i've made
in a long time.

but am i running from or running to?
or does the distinction even matter at this time?

journal entry: March 11, 2022

Getting close
to the day of departure.
i'm packing.
Repacking.
Unpacking and packing again.
Thinking of different ways to fit everything in...
How many pairs of socks?
Do i really need that shirt?
Which journal do i take?
How many journals is too many?
Is four too many? Probably.
The first aid kit was the first to be packed,
but even in there
i may have too much.
It weighs too much.
It's hard leaving things behind,
you wonder if you'll need it...
Will i need it? What if i do and don't bring it?
i go through, gram by gram, counting.
What do i take and what can i leave behind?

Let go and trust,
is what all the prep books have to say.

The Camino does provide,
doesn't it?
i'm hoping it does.

journal entry: March 23, 2022

One week
'til i leave for the Camino de Santiago.

One week
and i'll be gone for 50 days.

The longest
i've ever been away from home, from my kids,
so much longer on my own than i've ever been.

i'm nervous.
i'm anxious.
i'm excited.
i'm feeling the love and support all around,
from the Camino already
through ordering my credenciales,
a signature scallop shell for my pack to let everyone know
I'm a pilgrim too,
to friends and family offering help and wanting to know
more details.
At times i tear up thinking about it.
You'd think i'd be nervous about walking such a long way
by myself...
i thought i'd be more nervous about that too.
Surprisingly most of my nerves are about leaving my kids,
hoping they'll be fine with me gone.
My guilt - i'll be gone for so long!

Isn't that how it usually goes?
"They" make us moms feel guilty about leaving our kids,
even if only for a short time,
even if it's good for us and will feed our soul.
Society expects us to stay home
and do "what's best" for our kids.
But what if what's best for our kids
is that we get away for a while?
Is that so wrong?
Why do i feel like it's so wrong?

Why do i feel judgement from all around
in between all the love and support?
Hot and cold. Mixed signals.
Or is it displaced judgement from myself so i can blame
others and not have to look at one of my shadows that
follows me everywhere i go?

They'll be fine. i know they will.
(This will be good for all of us. i know it.)

i'm ready.
Ready to dive off the edge of the world
and into the arms of the universe.
The biggest, boldest swan dive i've ever dreamt of taking
into this unknown.
i'm ready.

i think...

journal entry: March 25, 2022

Now i know the universe doesn't conspire
to ruin your life
or do things to make your life turn upside down
for no reason,
but a couple of things have happened
that led me to wonder,
"What the hell, Universe!
Don't you know i'm leaving town soon?"

i know that just because something bad (or unwanted)
happens,
it doesn't mean the world is going to fall apart
as i know it.

But...

i got called for jury duty on a day when i'm going to be out of
the country AND I got into a heartbreaking argument with
my youngest.

It's selfish of me to want everything to be "just so"
before leaving.
There will never be a perfect time
for this or that.
There will always be threads undone,
tables not set.
if we wait for that perfect time,
we'll be waiting forever.
This i know.

i was able to reschedule my jury duty
and
my youngest and i worked through things.
(But does the mom guilt ever really go away?)

There's something else bothering me too...

Paul.

Not him personally
but the fact that he'll be joining me for a week
on the Camino.

Paul is a friend I've known since childhood,
and we've been dating for a few months now.
I adore our relationship.
Not only is he a beautiful friend,
but he's a caring lover, a giver
and has supported me in ways i haven't felt supported
in years.

He's so excited about this journey of mine and wants to walk
a few days with me.
And i am happy to share it with him...
When he first mentioned it, i thought,
Sure! That'd be so much fun!
But the more i think about it, the more i think...
i'm supposed to be doing this on my own.
This is my time. My journey. My healing path.
Sure, i'm excited to spend a few days in Europe with him,
but at the same time,
why can't i say, "No, this is my time,"
and trust he'll understand.

It feels i can't be trusted.
Or am i just creating this in my head...

—

My nerves about
the leaving and the being
on the Camino are beginning to get the best of me.
Or is it the other way around?
Am i getting the best of my nerves and allowing myself to do
what i do best...
unnerve me?

more

the more pictures i see, the more stories i hear,
the more "you should do this"
and "don't forget to take that" -
the more i create images in my head
of what i should expect, what i will experience, and
it's getting so overwhelming.
i need to stop.
stop researching.
stop the searching.
stop the "must make sure everything is correct
and everything will be okay,"
from running my mind.
there is no controlling this. the call.
it's bigger than me. it's its own being!
another life granting me
the life i've yet to discover.
it's time to let the universe take over.
it's time to let the Camino take over.
it has called
and i am ready.
i've done the research. i've packed.
what i need has been checked and packed,
double-checked and repacked.
i will be okay.
time to trust. trust in my decision. trust in my gut.

at some point, you have to ask yourself,
"what if it all works out?
what if all of my dreams do, indeed, come true?
who am i to not have dreams come true?
aren't i worthy of it, too?"

doubt

doubt
creeping up on you
in the darkest moments.

i can't seem to get through these
huge emotions.
they are taking over,
suffocating,
sweeping me out to sea,

there was a time i believed in fairytales.
no more.
i no longer believe Love will save all.
and isn't it sad...

everything i thought i knew
has been tossed and thrown out the door.

when i love someone, i give my all.
but how do you balance it all?
how do you keep your dreams afloat
and support someone else in a different boat?
how do you make sure you're not ships at night
crossing paths only to witness a few blinking lights?
i'm not sure i know how to be myself
with someone else.
(and i've got my kids to support, as well.)
how do you do this?
i was never taught that balance we all crave.
why was i never taught?

i am overwhelmed,
when i talk about my feelings, it's like i'm complaining
or burdening,
that he'll just get fed up and leave (just like Jude).
but then again, if he leaves, he leaves.
there's nothing i can do to stop him.
i know i'm a good person

and my feelings are valid too.
i am worthy of being loved as i choose to be loved,
just as he has chosen how (or not) to be loved.

i'm scared to be on my own.
but i'm scared to be in relationship.
i want to be held.
i want to be safe.
i want Paul's arms to hold me up
when i'm falling down.
but can i trust those arms?
why can't i trust those arms?
why do i doubt myself?
will i ever learn to trust myself?

what if you learn to fly?
what if you build wings on the way down?
what if you carry yourself
on the backs of those winds and create a soul-giving space
for you and someone else?
what if?

packing to unpack

i knew changing my outside would be easy.
job. things. pillow to sleep on. blanket to sleep with.
it's easy to travel halfway around the world and have
totally different surroundings to look at and be in.
but no matter the outside,
the inside remains the same.
forty-four years with my dad,
twenty-one years with my best friend,
eleven years with my (now ex) husband
are still there.
inside me.
there's a lot to unpack.
there's a lot to sift through.
there's a lot to unravel.

i know i'll have a hard walk climbing those mountains,
walking those long stretches of the Meseta,
navigating those forests,
but i am about to have an even harder walk
through memories and what-ifs that won't leave me
alone,
the agony and angst,
the tears and sorrow,
the dreams that will never come true
and the moments that will never be shared...

why

yes, the fear of being judged by others
for leaving my kids
and going away for a month and a half
is weighing heavily on me now.
what will they think?
the people i work with,
the friends who keep asking questions,
my siblings and the little competition held between us
of who's "better",
Paul, who thinks i'm going on an extended vacation,
and my mother,
my dear mother,
who is looking after my kids while i'm gone.
how can i make them see?
why do i need to make them see?
why don't they understand how much i need this?
why do we do this to each other?
why do we **not** support those closest to us in what is
calling our soul?
is it guilt? is it shame? is it jealousy? i don't
understand.
perhaps it's not for me to understand.
my job is not to figure everyone else out...
but that's what i learned growing up, right?
sort people out so that my surroundings are safe,
so no one argues,
no one yells,
keep the peace, be quiet,
don't be too loud
and "don't ruffle any feathers."
well, i'm done with that.
i'm ruffling feathers.
it's my turn to feed myself.
it's my turn to nurture my soul, because
honestly
**if i don't, these broken pieces within
may not (re)assemble again.**

the day before i left

i sat in my room,

my little
cramped
little room

at my mom's house
(where we moved after the divorce)
sending query after query
to literary agents and publishers,
hoping someone would bite and want to publish
my novel...

the novel that got me through this last year,

all its harrowing events
one after the other -
my father, my soul sister, my marriage.

i sent query after query, teary-eyed but hopeful
that someone would see the story
inside the byline...

sitting at my desk
computer open and music playing in the background,
all three kiddos came in to sit on my bed
to talk
to chat
to just be
and at some point,
all the pets were there too...
two cats and a dog
in a tiny
cramped
tiny, little bedroom.
but it was perfect.
so perfect.

my heart filled to the rim.
actually... it overflowed.

i could conquer the world
on this day.
i could cross oceans and climb mountains
on this day.
everything was okay,
yes
everything will be okay.

i asked my mom to make her delicious,
nobody-makes-em-like-she-does
cheese grits
and had the family "dinner"
i had been hoping to have
before leaving.

it was perfect.

the Body [45]

"And suddenly, you know it's time to start something
new and trust the magic of beginnings."

- Meister Eckhart

Starting in Saint Jean Pied de Port

journal entry: April 2, 2022

We traveled from Paris to St. Jean Pied de Port today,
Paul and i,
via train and bus.
It was a long day of travel.
Our second train was canceled
and we didn't know this until
we got to the station,
rushing around, pulling our stuffed packs onto our backs
only to find
no trains
in sight or even scheduled to arrive.

This was a foreign land with foreign words on a foreign
departure board next to our foreign destination...
In this part of France, the language is different.
It's not French and it's not Spanish. A sort of something in
between?

We followed the crowd,
trying to ask what that word meant,
that word up on the board
that lit steadily next to the train number we were supposed
to be on.
After seconds to minutes that felt like hours filled with worry
and dread,
we finally understood.
Thankfully, the town of Bayonne was prepared.
They had a bus waiting for us all,
ready
to take us to St. Jean.
Backpacks and all.

We threw everything in and jumped on.
i was too excited to talk.
All i wanted to do was

watch the mountains roll by in the distance,
those beautifully snow-covered mountains,
i said to him, "We have to cross those, you know."
He smiled a nervous smile.

His leg was bothering him.
It had been bothering him ever since Paris.
Since that one wrong turn that tweaked whatever muscle in
his leg and nearly paralyzed him in the moment.
i felt bad for him, i really did.
He wanted to walk with me, i knew he did.
And i was excited to walk with him too,
to experience some of the Camino with him -
this person who had helped me prepare and research and
shop for things that i needed,
like a backpack
that i shopped for and tried on and
walked around the store with
carrying weights to simulate what i'd be carrying
on my back for weeks and weeks,
and a sleeping bag
that i debated tirelessly over,
"do i really need it?... i don't know... maybe i do?"
this person whom i'd known for years and now had been
dating for a few months and felt
we had something good going,
this person whom i trusted and loved and
thought i was in love with...

But how far would he be able to walk, honestly?
His leg, it worried me,
as i knew it worried him too.
it was beginning to cause tension between us.
This, i knew.

We got off the bus, looked around, saw pilgrims going this
way and that, trying to find their place in the night as the
sun was quickly setting
and we were getting antsy.
i looked at the map,
at the name of the hostel i had booked for the night.

It was no where to be found.
The anxiety was building.
Where would we stay for the night?
Walking up the street,
trying to follow other pilgrims footsteps
for fear of getting lost.
we saw a lively little bar with people gathering outside.
Starved from our long journey from Paris,
we decided to check it out since
we'd have to eat something somewhere, anyway.
Why not here?

i started to hear "Buen Camino" from all around us
as we journeyed through the night
and my heart began to feel better.

We found a place to stay
by the grace of the gods,
by the grace of desperation,
by the grace of the Camino (i'd soon learn)
a hotel right on the trail overlooking this ancient path
so many pilgrims have started out on
so many years before us,
and now we were ready
to get up early in the morning and get going

...except for an argument
we really could've done without.

the pulling of the first thread

social media,
a sore spot in both of my marriages.
one thought i was cheating on him,
and the other, well,
not exactly, but similar.

i knew i wanted to share my journey
of this Camino
with friends and family
in various ways but through instagram,
mainly,
stories, posts, and inspirations
on the daily.

i am so often inspired by others online
and am grateful for their views and grace.
if i can't provide that grace to a stranger
by the time i leave here,
then i have arrived nowhere.

—

we were both tired,
exhausted from the day,
from the long, multiple train rides here
to searching for a place to stay.

Paul's leg was hurting
and i was sensitive to this,
he said he could use a massage
and i said i'd get to it,
but i wanted to write, i wanted to rest,
i wanted to share, i wanted to post,
to contemplate my journey ahead
without a myopic lens.
i wanted to expand my already expanding horizon
to allow everyone in,
my journey, to be witnessed was important

but all i felt was selfishness and judgement.

he didn't like it,
me spending time online, this night,
and made snide remarks
that only threw me further aside.
it didn't make me feel very good,
in all honesty, i wanted to run.
but i stayed in silence,
in tears 'til the rising sun
came up in the morning
when we packed and set out
on uneasy feelings, forcing smiles
and attempts to cross off any of the doubt.

that argument, we could've done without.
it was stupid, it was pointless,
when we should've been supporting each other
and feeling weightless.

all i wanted was to be seen and feel heard.

day 1 - SJPDP to Roncesvalles

the first steps

waking up before the sun to get a good breakfast
and our heads on straight
before starting out
on the long, long
24km (15mi) hike today...
because of our fight last night, neither of us were
feeling our best,
i knew i wasn't and i could tell
he wasn't either.

(i knew your leg was bothering you
and i wanted to help.
but i also, selfishly or not, wanted to be on my own and
walk this damn thing to free my mind of all that was
weighing it down.
that was my initial plan,
i was happy to have you here
to share in this experience,
but i began to feel something different,
something strange from you.
yes, i resented you for being here.
yes, i resented you for taking time to rest
when i wanted to walk further and faster.
yes, i resented you for adding more weight for me
to carry
when i felt the world was too much on my shoulders
already
pushing me further
and harder
into the ground
barely holding myself up for air,
clawing my way forward,
wanting to climb higher and higher to escape it all.)

we sat at a table in a quiet dining hall,

the first to arrive and dive into a breakfast i wouldn't
see again anywhere on the Camino -
(except in Pamplona at the Hotel la Perla).

i wanted to eat everything in sight, for i knew i'd need
the energy.
but my stomach was only so big and i didn't want to
risk cramps while hiking.
so i drank the freshly-squeezed orange juice, sipped
the warm-in-my-hands coffee, munched on a flaky
croissant with jam,
ate fresh fruit, ham and cheese, dried dates, and as
much of the cinnamon roll as i possibly could and
stared out the window
at this 12th century town
on the border of France and Spain
feeling like i'd stepped onto the set of a live action
Beauty and the Beast...

there weren't many pilgrims around,
we were just two of a few starting out.
nonetheless,
there was excitement in the air
with a little apprehension mixed in.
i sensed the tiniest bit of dread, but i tried desperately
to push it away,
for this was my journey and i didn't want anything to
taint it.

no need to do it all on your own, though...
for you are not alone.

on my own

we walked out from St. Jean Pied de Port
with the old stone buildings hugging tightly knitted
cobbled streets,
an idyllic medieval town in Basque Country, France
nestled at the foot of the Pyrenees,
"the foot of the pass"
for every pilgrim that starts this Way
the Camino Francés
backpacked
heading out
with eager hearts and spirited steps,
towards the mountains,
following the maps of the Pilgrim Office,
careful not to follow the hike towards the Napoleon
route, which was closed on this day...
for an unexpected amount of snow had just fallen.
we took note and followed "the rules",
passing grazing sheep and making new friends from
Germany to Australia
following the Way along winding roads, forests, and
streams
until we reached Valcarlos
...when he decided to take a taxi.

i was on my own.
disappointment held me in its arms,
yet i carried on.

me and the Pyrenees

i devoured my sandwich,
one of those deliciously long ham and cheese creations
we found
in a café in Paris before leaving.

i wasn't sure how much daylight i had
to walk from Valcarlos to Roncesvalles ...
it was only about noon, so nearly certain i'd be fine
but still
i was crossing the Pyrenees,
these mountains
that looked like any other mountain range but aren't.
these mountains
you read about in history books
and never think you'll touch but do.
these mountains
that hold greatness in their name,
amongst their winds weaving by,
within their enormity against the horizon
of a distant land,
their legend and lore,
and now in real life
under your feet and before your eyes.

i was nervous and wanted to get going,
i didn't want to leave him behind
but then again, i wanted to leave him behind
(not in a mean way),
i wanted to get walking,
start climbing,
seeing everything there was to see.
i had that spirit in my step,
the same spirit we saw in fellow pilgrims
back in St. Jean,
a smile on their faces
and a quickness in their walking sticks.
there was a call to my soul and
an urge to climb those mountains

i wanted to run, to soar through them
to conquer them
to name them mine
to feel my boots make their mark
with each and every step
over rock and gravel...

trust and climb

the snow was calling me.
the trees were calling me.
the birds flew higher and higher,
beckoning me to follow.
"you'll see!" they cried.
i trusted and climbed.

the first day is the hardest

i pursued fresh footsteps beyond a yellow ciudado line
and thought,
"maybe they just forgot to take this one down?"
the yellow Camino arrows were pointing in that
direction...
not up the paved road
which the Pilgrim Office maps said to take today,
but down a veering narrow stone path...
and because of the fresh boot-prints, i trailed the same.
it wasn't until deep in the forest, higher up the
mountain
that i wondered if i'd made the right decision...
i remembered the man in the Pilgrim Office
warning us about the snow,
warning us not to go "that way"...
"stick to the road," he said. "there's been an unusual
amount of snowfall lately, it's too dangerous."
but the arrows were there,
the fresh footsteps were there,
and to be honest, my stubbornness was there
right beside me.
too late now. can't go back. i have to continue this way,
following these
yellow arrows that soothed every doubt in my mind
that i was going the wrong way,
almost hidden by snow but appearing when i needed
them.

and more snow was beginning to fall!
"if it keeps up like this, i'm screwed," i thought.

each step grew more laborious with
the snow gripping onto my trekking poles and boots,
weighing me down,
each breath a complete effort
in its own time.
nothing else mattered but that next step.
one more step to get me to Roncevalles.

one more step to get me over these mountains.
one more step to prove that i can do it.
but as i continued to climb,
i looked up into the mountains and saw how much much
further
i had to go.
just breathe
and climb.
breathe
and climb.
the repetition reminded me of yoga, honestly.
that time i joined in
on an excruciating 108 sun salutations to celebrate the
coming of Spring
(oh spring! what i'd give to have warm toes right now!)
and those times in class, exhausted but wanting to hold
on just a little bit longer
to find my breath,
to find my strength.
those moments were coming back to me with each
falling snowflake
that landed on nearby branches,
building the piles of snow and growing in strength,
reminding me to breathe.
just breathe.
i saw a bird or two flying high
and it reminded me of Dad.
he loved to sit outside and watch the birds
(and so did i).
i felt a tailwind jostle my back
as if it was a friend encouraging me to keep going
(Kym, is that you?)
reminding me to breathe.
just breathe,
as i moved further up the mountain, stone after stone,
step after step,
my boots following in the previous hiker's footsteps
hoping to make my thighs a little happier with less
effort
but still,
my poles stuck in the snow and held me back.

more snow dropped as if a million dandelions had been
awakened
reminding me to breathe.
"just breathe" came through the winds,
just as it has many times before
when i needed to hear it.

when things get tough,
breathe.
when expectations feel too heavy,
breathe.
when the uncertainty of what's next
tightens every muscle in your body,
breathe.
when single-parenthood grows exhausting,
breathe.
when life floods the clarity in your mind,
breathe.
when bank accounts empty too fast,
breathe.
when you're tired from not sleeping well,
breathe.
there is comfort in the breath.
there is comfort in difficult postures,
there is comfort in the hard moments,
if you breathe.
just breathe...

those footsteps that looked so fresh
were defiant hikers like me.
those yellow arrows that led the way to Roncesvalles
were the guidance i needed to get me there.
that drive in my heart repeating, "you got this!"
was what pulled me forward.
i cried.
i laughed.
i cursed.
i talked to myself
and
i cried again.
wondering what the hell i was doing.

will i make it out of here?
"shit, it's snowing again... will i lose my way?
...and if i do, will someone find me?"

the mountains climbed higher and higher,
still.
the snow grew deeper and deeper,
still.
the sun shone lazier and lazier,
still,
hiding behind clouds.
making my way through the forest and trees more dim
more unnerving,
and more tiring.

they say the first day is the hardest.
24 kilometers/15 miles from SJPDP to Roncesvalles.
i heard and
understood
every word of this over-repeated phrase of advice,
"the first day is the hardest."
(but did i really?)
they're right.
it is the hardest...
so far.
i just didn't realize how "hardest" would feel

on

every

inch

of my being.

i didn't realize how "hardest" would challenge me
physically
step after step,
higher and higher
into those mountains that seemed to go on forever.
twisting here,

hiding there
in forests that make you think the light
on the other side
is the end of your trail today...
these mountains that have claimed lives before me
and would likely claim more after.
this, kept replaying in my head,
reminding me to breathe,
just breathe.
thighs burning
chest pumping
lungs grasping for energy with every inhale
holding on to thinning air
out of awe from the beauty around.
but if i held my breath, would i find it
at the next turn
when the scenery changed?
or would i find it harder to breathe,
because i haven't let myself exhale?

i continued to place my increasingly-heavy boots
step by step
into the snow, knee-deep in parts,
along the path i followed but wasn't supposed to,
one that called my name
as if it were a game of Marco Polo,
i'm right here... you just have to find me.

but would i find you?

this "hardest" day was tough physically
but mentally as well...
overcoming those doubts
those fears
that rollercoaster ride from elation to sorrow,
energy to exhaustion
and back again.
the breathtaking views of a landscape that could
swallow you whole
without doubt or remorse,
the negative self-talk that came so easily

just like the night
when you questioned every detail of what you thought
went wrong...

but somehow,
someway,
the Camino finds you.
the Camino calls and guides you
into its realm of possibility and encourages you
to strengthen a weakening physical body
and psyche
with each and every heavy boot into and out of the
snow
behind a handful of others who had trekked before me
today,
(and thank God they had,
for i wouldn't have made it out, if it wasn't for them).

you are safe. you are loved. keep going,
for i am at your back and in the birdsong above.

roncevalles

i made it to Roncesvalles.

the monastery rounding the corner after a long, hard
trek through rock and snow
was a sight to ease all nerves,
all sores,
all the pieces of this jagged heart,
and a spirit so torn.

but i made it.
Paul was there
waiting at the door.
smile on his face and relief in his heart.
he had already checked in and chosen a bunk next to
the new Swedish friends he'd met in Valcarlos -
Mats and Monica -
with warm smiles and thick Scandanavian accents
they welcomed me too.
they knew more English than i did Spanish,
putting this American to shame,
but so lovingly accepted me into their Camino world
and invited me along their way so many times over
that they became
two of my most cherished Camino friends,
keeping in touch even after our physical walks ended.

i guess Paul had told everyone how worried he was
about me, because
everyone was so happy to see me.
even the hospitaleros said when stamping my
credenciales,
"he's been so worried."
this (re)filled my heart where it had poured out
over the mountain.
with an exhausted smile and tears in my eyes,
i rushed off to shower, then dinner, then to bed.
no time to journal.
no time to think.

just time for a few hugs, some wine and pasta.
barely time to check in with my kids.
was i a good mom for coming all the way here?
guilt was still residing.

i only hoped i would inspire them to do what calls their
heart.

day 2 - Roncevalles to Zubiri

¡buenos días!

"¡buenos días!" the hospitaleros said with cheer as they
turned on the lights and urged everyone up and out the
door.

8 o'clock. we must be out by 8 o'clock...
everyone else was nearly out the door.
i felt slow.
i'd never done this before,
questioning myself, "what am i forgetting? am i
forgetting anything?"
i had already left my phone charger and outlet adapter
back in Paris
and raced around the train station to find another,
i can't leave it again.
it's my link to the outside world! what if i get lost? what
if something happens and i need to call someone?
i checked and double-checked
...it's in my bag, as is my passport and money.
all good.
i stuffed everything back in my pack,
including my sleeping bag that takes forever to stuff
back in
but will turn out to be one of my most cherished items
on the trail.
(thanks Paul!)

we're out the door and
it's cold. it's snowing. but the beauty is soul-opening.
walking through the ancient courtyard of the
monastery blanketed in snow,
we stop to take photos of the rising sun
over fields of white
in between trees asleep in the arms of winter's
embrace.
i risk sending my fingers into Raynaud's numbness for

photos of everything around me.
walk walk walk, click.
walk walk walk, click.
Paul is tiring of me stopping here and there for photos,
but in all honesty...
it fits his pace.
his leg is still bothering him
but he's determined to make it.
21.5 kilometers/13 miles
i'm aching from yesterday but i'm determined to make
it too.
"Zubiri" is all we hear.
the next stop.
"where are you stopping? we're stopping there."

i haven't yet fallen into the pace of the Camino...
the stop-when-you-need-to pace,
the go at your own rhythm that comes later down the
way,
so i follow the crowd.

to Zubiri

we follow the path
through snowy forests, icy roads,
small towns, hills and valleys,
i slip on black ice and hurt nothing but my ego.
brush it off, laugh
take a photo and move on.
it's quiet out here.
nothing but the trees and their silent sleep
through winter,
horses grazing gently through patches of white,
finding grass between blankets of frost,
they look up at us in curiosity, then head back down
to mind their own business.

walk walk walk
stop for a café con leche y plátano
in a tiny, sleepy shop
then walk
walk
walk again...

the trek down
into Zubiri
can only be described as torturous excitement.
excitement because you're almost there but
torturous on the knees and legs,
mind and soul.
vertically laden slats of rock made by some trickster or
devil? you wonder,
trying to trip you up or bring doubt to your mind
(it was working too)
in this stretch
it was way too easy to step wrong or sprain an ankle,
possibly break something - so
step after step
never looking up
ever so careful to place each foot exactly so
where it won't rebel

and
twist
down
into the grooves.

(hiking down is so much harder than climbing up.)

journal entry: April 4, 2022

i wish i had journaled yesterday in Roncevalles
but i was exhausted.
And with barely any time between checking in, finding my
bed, showering and rushing to dinner,
i was asleep without any energy to pick up a pen.

i'm sore.
My legs hurt this morning
and are so sore tonight from today.
But they're a sore i've never experienced before.
It feels good to hurt like this,
to feel the aches inside every bone and every muscle,
knowing this is what carried me
30 miles in two days, with 20 pounds on my back.
My body.
My wonderful body.

Just when you think you can't go a step further,
Spirits around you start showing up
Dad
Kym
all the pilgrims before me
all the ones who will come after me
they send a tailwind,
a bird,
or a soft falling of snow...
They're here, i feel them guiding me on.

i'm looking forward to being on my own.
It's fun with Paul here.
It's nice to share this with the one you love.
...but i'm supposed to be doing this on my own
to let go
to break and (re)build
That's why i'm here.
How am i supposed to do that when i'm worried about
someone else?
If he'll make it... Is he okay?... Is he angry?... What can i do

to make it better?...
Nothing.
There's nothing i can do to make things better.
It is what it is.
His body can't make the journey, nor was it ever meant to.
He has responsibilities at home and i understand that. i
know he'll be there when i get back...

...or at least i think he will.

day 3 - Zubiri to Pamplona

breakfast in Zubiri

Paul went down to the dining room
before me...
he had decided to take a taxi to Pamplona
due to his injury,
so no need to hurry and pack his stuff.
he grabbed a seat for him and me at one of the three
long farm tables
that fed the hungry pilgrims before setting out to walk.

i was grateful for him,
talking, chatting with all those around us,
making friends
when i was too introspective to hold conversations.

he chose seats across from Mats and Monica,
next to Bekah,
a talkative girl with a dark-haired bob
and a can do! attitude.
she told all of us
at the breakfast table
of that one thing she was trying to conquer on this
adventure...
"what's the one thing you didn't treat yourself to
but wish you had?
for instance, right now
at breakfast,
are you holding back from having one more pastry?"
she asked.
it made me think...

just as my brother told me when i talked to him about
taking so many pictures...
"you'll never get this moment back. why not take as
many pictures as you'd like? PLUS, it gives you a
moment to breathe. and we all know how important

that is."
(so true, Patrick.)

so true, Bekah.
yes!
i will take that second pastry, thank you!

"for me, it's more butter on my toast this morning,"
Bekah told the table
and proudly reached for her knife and the butter dish.

Bekah was a pastor on her own pilgrimage
of self-discovery.
was this the road she was supposed to be taking?
she explained.
she felt the need to test it out...
just like she did with the church she joined back home
when she dressed in the rattiest clothing after not
showering for days, no brush through her hair and dirt
beneath her fingernails,
she entered the church and sat down,
waiting
to be asked to leave or
to be welcomed.
when she was welcomed and handed a bulletin,
she knew it was the place for her.

Suzanne was Bekah's friend.
a little less enthusiastic but helpful to anyone in need.
Suzanne and i bonded immediately over our
matching backpacks.
our red Gregory's that
faithfully carried
each of our lives
day after day
all the way.

while putting on my boots after breakfast
and getting ready to "hit the road,"
Suzanne asked if i needed any band-aids
or blister medication.

"no, i think i'm good,"...
then i thought of the little spot
on my heel
that was beginning to get a little irritated.
my first aid kit was already packed tightly in my bag.
"on second thought," i reached out to Suzanne,
"i think i will take a band-aid. thanks!"

bandage on,
foot cream, socks, and boots on,
we took a photo
Suzanne, Bekah, and me
with our Gregory packs in sisterhood,
ready to take the path out of Zubiri
towards Pamplona.

i left about 30 minutes before they did
and learned later that night
that Paul had offered to send snacks with them
for me,
but being 30 minutes ahead,
the likelihood of them catching up
was slim.

(why can't i see the care people offer in the moment?)

why does it take climbing mountains
for me to believe them?

meeting my first angels

i walked out of the albergue in Zubiri with a
bittersweet spark in my heart.
Paul stayed back to pack and call a taxi to Pamplona.
i am out on my own.
21 kilometers/13 miles
blue skies
very little snow starts off the morning then dissolves
into luscious green grasses and trees,
rivers and streams alongside me nearly the whole way
some slow and peaceful
others rushing and racing over rocks and branches,
equally beautiful.
the last of the ice and frost with
everything turning a fresh new green,
lit and warmed by the rising sun.

the steep climb into Arleta and on to Trinidad de Arre
was long and challenging -
i was so hungry and wondered if i'd make it to a café
for something to eat.
faint and tired,
reaching for more gum
to squeeze whatever sugar out of it
to keep me going.

but just as skies clear when you're flooding from rain,
the Camino opens up...

a man appeared in the middle of the forest, high on the
hilltop i was climbing
with a table and a tarp
draped for shade,
baskets of fruits and juices
ready for the hungry.
a God-send. a Camino-send!
i bought a lemonade and una naranja and replenished
my soul.
just what i needed to get me to Trinidad de Arre for

some lunch.

some arduous kilometers later,
i ate next to a couple in a café with a 9-month-old
baby girl.
"we want her to be able to say she walked her Camino
before she could even walk," they said.
talk about trusting the Way and being forced to take
your time!
there's no hurrying a 9-month-old...

with my hunger satiated and my thirst quenched,
i carried on.
tired but better.
my feet starting to ache in places new and unnerving.
when can i get these boots off?
is it the distance?
is it because it's day 3 and i'm exhausted?
whatever it is, these paved streets between Trinidad de
Arre and Pamplona are hard on the feet and harder on
the soul,
for there's so much time to think in all the
thought-space that shows up
in these long stretches of aloneness and quiet,
processing why you're (i'm) here.

as i was coming into the town of Pamplona, a
grey-haired man
stopped me to say, "buen Camino"
(he oddly reminded me of the most southern
gentleman, world-renowned surgeon, i used to work
for and i smiled. is this a coincidence?)
he asked where i was from and "why a person so young
as you comes to walk el Camino? and alone?"
such sincerity burst my heart wide open
and i nearly fell into tears
right then and there.

"i'm walking for my dad.
i'm walking for my best friend.
i'm walking to (re)gain some sense of life

after yet another divorce.
i'm walking for myself, for some peace, some clarity,
some new view on life
rather than the inside-out version i've been locked into
over the past year or so,"
is what i wanted to say.
but it didn't come out quite as eloquently as that.

he asked if i was religious,
and at this point all i could say was, "i'm very spiritual.
i grew up episcopalian but no longer participate in it."
i never felt judged in his presence.
he listened with an open heart and a beautiful smile.
offered kind words of encouragement and a prayer for
my journey.
"God bless you. he is always with you. you are not
alone," he said.
i cry even now
thinking of those words from that gentle man.
we hugged, exchanged names, and i asked for a photo.
i wanted to remember this angel of my Camino for all
my days to come.

in tears
was how i walked the rest of the way into Pamplona.
right into the hotel where Paul was standing, waiting
patiently to take my walking sticks and help me
upstairs.
i wouldn't let him take my pack -
it was a part of me now.
so was this story that i kept so close to my heart,
so close that i couldn't even talk about it.
i showered and Paul rubbed my back with lotion.
we sat in silence for a moment or two,
then went downstairs to meet up with Mats and
Monica, the Swedes,
and grab a bite to eat.

these two men on the path today helped me more than
they'll ever know.

just when you think you're alone ... something or someone comes along to help.

a prayer

On my way to Santiago,
I want to enjoy walking.
If You are there, You are also here, by me,
while walking.
Help me to become a reality, my dreams, my
hopes, and my projects.
I want to be thankful and to respect the views
of others,
making together a better world.
While walking, give me the gift of finding in
those who make the walking, true brothers and
sisters.
May I grow among those who make the Way
the kinship spirit.

-- given to me by my Angel of the Camino
in Pamplona on this day

day 4 - rest day in Pamplona

rest

today is a rest day.
in Pamplona,
at the Hotel la Perla, Hemingway's favorite place to
stay when in this town.
it is beautiful. almost too beautiful,
too luxurious
too indulgent for this pilgrim on the Camino, i thought
but it's nice
and Paul is here and we're
having a breakfast spread like i've never seen before.
trays bigger than your lap
full of breads, sweet and savory,
cheeses
jams and meats.
there are also sidebars
filled to the edges with coffees, teas, orange juice, and
cereals,
eggs, bacon, more cheeses, breads, pastries, and more...
we feasted while we wrote,
me in my journal and him on his postcards for family
until we were stuffed and couldn't stomach
another bite.
what we didn't eat, we packed and took with us.
him, for his journey back to Paris then home
and me, for my continued journey along the Camino
when the trail was promised to grow long and
strenuous with no tiendas around.

after breakfast, we walked around Pamplona.
stopped to load a washer in a lavandería for a proper
clothes cleaning,
shopped for more comfortable shoes for both of us
(i needed a pair of sandals that i could wear with socks
because
1... it's cold

and 2... my boots were the last thing i wanted to wear
when i arrived in an albergue, showered and in
for the night),
toured the cathedral,
then met up with Mats and Monica for dinner at
another of Hemingway's haunts -
Café Iruña.

but all this indulgence was about to end...

damn the night

after all the loss i had just been through,
i never expected to receive more.
not here.
not on the Camino
where i was supposed to be (re)filled to the top from
being empty for so long,
not after i had learned to trust someone
again
just to be let go of like a balloon in the sky, admired
but no longer wanted around your wrist.
sure i wanted to do this walk on my own,
(that was always the intention from the moment i told
you about it)
to be supported, to be held, even from a distance
to have a partner who understood.
i never expected you to end things here in Europe.
here in Pamplona.
the day before you left to go back home.
was it that German girl?
was it something i said?
was it something i did or didn't do?
these questions ran through my head
over and around and upside-down
until it drove me crazy, thinking...
i'm just like this dust on the floor
these pebbles beneath my feet
these pigeons searching for scraps lying around,
anything from the over-indulgent diners who made
their way so carelessly
through the restaurant,
maybe one tiny piece will fall from their lips or laps?
it doesn't matter. it's all the same.

why did it hurt so bad?
why did i feel crushed yet again?
even though we said we'd remain friends,
it felt like another loss to add to my list of "to let go".
and what's worse?

he suggested we keep it to ourselves to "save" the kids
from any hurt for a while.
shit, i'm close to my kids. they're going to see right
through me.
the whole world is going to see right through me.
i wear my heart on my sleeve.
i cannot hold hard emotions in,
i can't hold anything in,
though it seems that way because i'm quiet...
i breathe and write
and breathe again
until whatever is stuck
escapes like a flood on paper,
until whatever i'm feeling
forms white horses on an ocean,
obvious and revealing
expressive and releasing
breaking open
only to the salt air above.

i can't do this,
it isn't fair.
i can't hide what i'm feeling,
i have to talk it out with someone,
but who?

Kym, where are you?

my brother answered the midnight call.

just go

don't sugarcoat it.
rip the bandage off.
no need to draw it out, i get it.
i'm here to reset my life
i know i want to do this on my own
but you were my friend
my lover
the one i called when i needed to vent
or cry
or laugh
or cheer.
i knew your kids and you knew mine.
i understood your past life,
you understood mine.
i gave into you and gave you my all,
now all i have is this falling apart.
i liked having you around,
i liked you in my life
but not like this,
not "just friends"
not in "we'll see…"
i can't keep you around like this.
i come first now
i come first here,
as i've been trying to do
ever since i packed my first pair of wool socks into
this damn backpack.
it's my turn.
time to love
myself.
time to realize
i'm not broken.
time to realize
it's not me, it's you.
"there are no rules to this. whatever you need."
bullshit.
stop with the terms of endearment.
stop with the nicknames

and encouraging affirmations.
you're breaking my heart
over again and under and around.
please stop.
i need space.
you chose this.
you wanted to leave.
just go.

she'd rather go than simply fade away.

day 5 - Pamplona to Puente la Reina

currents

i didn't get much sleep last night,
through the tears and positioning myself as far away in
the bed as i could,
i wrapped around a pillow and tried to imagine myself
somewhere else,
anywhere else but here...
i couldn't wait for the morning
to get up, dress, pack, and leave.

we ate breakfast in silence.
he asked for a text from me when i got to my next town.
i held it together and agreed,
for a ridiculous part of me hoped he'd change his mind.

it was time for me to start walking,
so we hugged
i cried and felt my heart falling into a deep dark river,
i was lost.

let the currents take me where they will.
i am at their mercy now.

the cards of the deck

there were more people on the trail today than i
thought would be,
like players around a roulette table,
from Pamplona to Alto del Perdón -
all vying for the same position and caring less about
the person standing near.
pilgrims, yes
but more annoyingly, kids on a school field trip
blasting music and climbing to the top as i was.
sure, "your Camino, your way"
but damn, be respectful of others' space.
i walked slower to let them pass.
no sense in fighting a tide
that was coming in regardless.
no sense in arguing with a player
who insists they know all the rules.
so i held back
and saw Mats and Monica.
oh thank God,
friends,
those beautifully strong Scandinavian souls who
taught me the right way to use my trekking poles.
nothing like a Swede to teach a Floridian how to
climb (or descend) a mountain.

i could really use some friends right now.

they mentioned Paul,
today's nine of clubs,
and i acted like everything was fine.
i wanted to tell them everything,
show my hand, throw my cards in,
i wanted to scream it all out to them
i wanted to cry
i wanted to blame
but i held my cards close,
i kept quiet,
for it was not their game to play.

it was mine.
for i was used to games of solitaire
when no one was around to see the cards fall.
i was used to patching up my ego
and catching my own tears
when defeat was in the shadows,
not for everyone everywhere.
they were on their journey
and i was on mine.

**sometimes it's easier to lose
when no one knows the game.**

we are never truly alone

somewhere
along the Way
this day
i met Jacey...
this vibrant gorgeous woman who
came upon me as i was making my way
to and from Alto del Perdón.

you ever have one of those friends?
they come out of nowhere and
conversations start mid-sentence,
like you've been talking for a lifetime
already?

meet Jacinda -
"you can call me Jacey," she said.

i could hear the Canadian accent in her voice
right away
and felt her strength and care through
each and every word,
feeling right at home in her presence.

we told each other our stories,
answering that all-too-common question
that came through the air
like the wingbeats of a bird,
"so, what brought you to the Camino?"
...catching each other's tears in our hearts
with reassuring words.

nowhere else
on this planet
can you tell your story to strangers
and feel heard
and held
and understood,
no matter what you say.

though you may be playing a game of solitaire,
there are numerous cards in the deck.
we are never truly alone.

92

finding my rhythm

Alto del Perdón was everything i imagined and more.
for it was one of the many historic sights
i read about before coming,
i just didn't expect its
magnitude.

the long hike
up to those tall, iron figures,
those pilgrims before me
with packs on their backs
and mules walking alongside too
one after the other, all in a line,
climbing this alto to reach a turbulent height of stones
and winds
only to descend
after a short rest among
a magnificent mountain
surrounded by endless horizons and skylines
with tall, powerful wind turbines
gathering the energy that wasn't being inhaled
by us pilgrims,
or vice versa -
perhaps we pilgrims were exhaling energy
into the winds
feeding those carefully sculpted fine white blades,
circling
in the blue sky.

there was enormous gratitude up on that hill.
an ethereal Grace,
a curiosity to delve into history.
what else happened up on
that hill?

how many others came before me
and how many would climb after?

there was a feeling there of a never-ending flow of

happiness and heartache,
pilgrim after pilgrim,
year after year.

these strong, iron pilgrims
frozen in time
standing tall on this mountain
were a sign of what may come...
strength.
endurance.
compassion.
maybe legacy too?
time will tell.

down from that alto,
Mats and Monica and i
found an albergue for the night
in Puente la Reina, where
one of the pilgrims was already making himself
at home
on the piano.
something soft,
something soothing,
i couldn't place the composer...
but i knew it from my childhood.

a child brought up
with classical music playing throughout the house
on sundays
and when i was in Charleston visiting family.

so many memories were flooding back,

and this time it was my grandfather
and his love
of poetry and classical music.
he died when i was 8
and i never got to tell him how much he meant to me.
but i imagine he knows,
for whenever i hear classical music
or play the piano myself,

i feel him there.

thanks for walking with me, JK.
i feel you here.

after showering and playing with the hospitalera's dog
who loves pilgrims
(this ball of energy came pouncing up the stairs to find
us all and give her love to the new people in her house
for the night)
we found a lovely bar,
a bottle of vino tinto,
and a nice dinner to follow.

fuel for the morning,
as we headed further down the path
across the Queen's Bridge
built in the 11th century,
down a path paved by many
for thousands of years.

day 6 - Puenta la Reina to Villatuerta

the first 100km

i left Puenta la Reina and soon
caught up with Jacey.

the first 100km -
we made it this far!
hard to believe.
we celebrated with a stop and a rest
and, of course, a selfie to document the moment.

after sitting for a while
on a short, stone wall with other pilgrims
chatting and sipping water
embracing the fresh air around us full of inspiration
and hope,
we continued on.

we passed a herd of horses
grazing peacefully in the hills,
bells jingling from around their necks,
oh those sleigh bells...
serene and magical,
like we had traveled back in time before big machinery
and
the patriarchy
where women held witchy powers
of healing and protection.
they guided our way down the road.

ethereal.

journal entry: April 8, 2022

i stopped in Villatuerta for the day.
The wind was brutal walking from Lorca to here
and my feet were absolutely killing me.
i saw an albergue that i remembered reading about
(they cook you dinner AND breakfast)
so i knocked on their door
and who comes smiling from over the railing?
Jacey!
Or as Mats loves to say, CANADA!!

i love how paths weave back and forth on this journey.
We started the day together but got separated,
as happens on the Camino.

Jacey and i met today on the stretch out from Pamplona.
We exchanged stories and connected from the start.
Sweet as can be and strong, oh so strong!
She's got legs on her that can carry faster and farther than
mine ever could.

This albergue feels like a hug
a much needed hug,
it's quiet and clean, respectful and modest
with stone walls and wooden floors.
Only 33 euros for a bed, dinner (4 courses with wine!), and
breakfast.
i'm so glad i stopped here and didn't push through to Estella.

No need to push through
when your body is saying otherwise.

the comfort of now

sitting at one of the beautiful wooden tables
in this quaint dining space
writing,
warm timber all around being lit by the cooling sun
relaxing the afternoon away,
listening to the hospitaleros making dinner
just behind the floral curtain separating me
from the kitchen.
i make a cup of rooibos tea
and one of them brings me a plate of sweet crackers.
the generosity is beyond all compare here.
the smells from the kitchen
as they cook
are making me hungrier by the second.
and their chatter in Spanish
with their little one coming in and out
is a comfort that soothes my soul after a
very hard, emotional start this morning.

Paul, i still don't understand
but i know i must let go.
it's hard
so hard for me.
my mind ruminates every conversation
every argument
every time we were together and i wonder
what happened.
but this, i know is perhaps not for me
to know.
it's the letting go of needing to know that's hard.

closure.
an unworthy opponent.
best to be here in the now,

breathe in this comfort
and let others simply be.

less is more

the three of us
in a room for six,
me and Jacey at one end
and little Miss Crinkly trying to fix
her silver, heated blanket
that looks like aluminum foil at the other.
i wonder how she's doing,
like really doing it all.
she seems a little unprepared
for the long haul ahead of us,
in conversations had right before dinner,
we offer advice and comfort her.
she joins our table,
as does Lars from Holland,
and sits quietly and listens
as Lars goes on and on about his medicine.
walking for health,
yes i do very much agree,
but he gives little room for conversation
and makes me wish it was only us three
again in the room
like it was before dinner,
when i was wondering about Miss Crinkly
and writing in silence, so much finer.

day 7 - Villatuerta to Los Arcos

un buen día

just when you think you've seen all the beauty the
Camino has to offer
another gorgeously breathtaking view
comes 'round the corner.

the walk today was pure beauty,
some ups, some downs
and most definitely, some tough parts.

i saw my first poppies though!
red poppies,
three of them
so beautiful.
i remember the packets of
red poppy seeds
at Kym's funeral, so
seeing these poppies alongside me today
brought huge smiles to my face.
(hi Kym, nice to have you with me today.)

the people i crossed paths with
along the Way today in Luquin
were so nice -
a sweet farmer working his hands into the earth smiled
and waved,
another local stopped me along the Way to ask
where i was from and
where i was headed,
Santiago de Compostela!
he spoke only Spanish and i only understood a bit
but we had a small conversation, filled with smiles
and heart.

meaningful, all the welcomes we receive as pilgrims.

journal entry: April 9, 2022

a good day of hiking.
22 kilometers/14 miles from Villatuerta to Los Arcos.
The weather was beautiful
and my feet didn't hurt too much,
though i was anxious to get my boots off
even just halfway through the day...
i have a blister on one of my pinky toes that's working its
way into a
helluva good one.

i arrived in Los Arcos around 3pm
found an albergue, checked in, showered, washed my
clothes, hung them out to dry (though it's cold and all the
drying lines in the sun are taken... i may have to pack them
up damp tomorrow and dry them at my next stop)
Mats and Monica are in the Plaza Mayor having wine...
"see you soon, guys! i'll be out in just a sec."

i'm sitting here, journal in lap
on my top bunk for the night
wondering if i'll get any sleep tonight...
Last night's sleep was delightful.
Just three of us females
No snorers, pure delight.
Tonight?
Doesn't look to be panning out in the same luck...
All men so far, i haven't seen a single girl,
Stinky feet and snorers -
is it tomorrow yet?
i also just received my first rejection letter for my novel.
Bummed, yeah.
i knew it would happen,
i mean, it's par for the course right?
Just keep plugging away...

Fingers crossed, it'll happen.

abundance, it's a perspective

i closed my journal
and hopped down from my bunk,
grabbed my shoes and jacket to meet
Mats and Monica in the square
for a little vino before turning in.

"where are you from?"
Lars from Holland asked as i was heading out.
when i said, "the United States,"
he looked surprised and said he thought i was
"one of them."
with the Pippi braids and fair, pale skin
many were thinking i was from the Netherlands.
hardly anyone expected me to say, "Florida."

i had my phone in hand
with my popsocket popped out for easy grip.
Lars laughed and asked, "what's that?"
"what, you don't have these where you're from?"
i asked.
he reached for my phone and examined it with
childlike wonder.

we, Americans, are over-indulgent, aren't we?
there's so much we could do without,
making the world a better place
if we did.
plastic, things, gadgets,
they're in abundance everywhere
in the States.
the grocery stores...
oh don't get me started on
the grocery stores.
do we really need it all?
aisles and aisles of chip selections,
spaghetti sauce options,
buckets of paper products to choose from...
in my honest opinion, we do not.

time on the Camino
will show you exactly
what you can live without.

rioja

olive trees and grape vines,
like little soldiers in a row.
planted and arranged with equal margins
centered beneath the sun above.

a disciplined visual arrangement,
beautifully sculpted by people and Spirit alike.

is there really a way to control life?
the rioja beauty makes you believe so.

day 8 - Los Arcos to Logroño

a lost day

from Los Arcos to Logroño
not much is written in my journal,
perhaps to exhaustion
perhaps to heartache...
a lost day.

i'm missing Paul
and what i thought we had.
there's a heaviness in my chest
and a burdensome weight on my back.
the Camino has seen so many of my tears
and has graciously caught them in the palm
of her hands,
providing comfort along the way.
as she continues
to hold my feet firm and encourage me to walk forward.
onwards and upwards, she whispers... *you've got this.*

i'm not sure at what point
my pack began to feel
like a part of me,
but the noises she was making today sounded so much
like a horse,
or riding horseback,
that i decided to give her a proper name...
Georgina.
she's red with a lot of attitude
(a little like me, you might say).
quite the pair, an extension of me,
Georgina, the beaut!
as belonging as my broken-in boots
or my trustworthy glasses i wear at night
in the dark.
i don't feel her weight anymore.
i don't feel her taut straps squeezing just so,

she's a part of me and i'm a part of her.
a lifeline or a heartbeat,
no breadth to divide,
worlds colliding and becoming one
to breathe.

i decided to eat lunch
under a tree in the grass
just outside of Viana,
the next city to walk through.
good thing too!
because there was a huge festival going on
with people crowding every street i looked down,
each café packed full
until people were sitting on windowsills and hanging
over the edge.

getting closer to Logroño... is that Sweden i see??
Mats and Monica!
"click click, click click," their walking sticks go.
a sight for sore, puffy eyes indeed.
they tell me where they're staying and i decide to stay
there too
much to the disappointment of Lars of Holland,
"Pippi!"
(my Camino nickname's starting to stick)
he invited me to share an airbnb in Logroño
but i didn't want to.
"No thank you."
i'm flattered... I mean,
no make-up and smelly from hardly a shower?
yes, i'm flattered, but still
no thanks.

after a lovely dinner with Mats and Monica,
we went back to our albergue and discussed what time
to start in the morning.
this town and this hostel -
not like the others i've been in so far.
it feels distant and
withdrawn, cold,

a line scribbled outside the circle, un-encompassing of
the warmth and spirited energy of days previous,
alien, you might say.
strange to me.
the albergue was dark with multiple rooms of
bunkbeds,
a central dull meeting room with couches and chairs
that i sat in to journal,
but the air was stale and
not a smile to walk by.

i will not miss Logroño
and its supposed constant state of celebration
that seemed to miss my night's quarters completely.

**but perhaps it's not Logroño's lack of life
i'm missing,
perhaps it's mine.**

day 9 - Logroño to Navarrete

ducks and new friends

leaving Logroño
we walked until we reached a lake
surrounded by locals and pilgrims alike
admiring the morning
the slight chill in the air
the sunshine beaming through the clouds
and mallards...
mallards swimming peacefully, gracefully
and i think of Dad.
he'd love to be here,
sitting
watching the ducks
in this cool spring air.

Mats and Monica introduce me to Stephanie,
from Germany,
as she walks up with a friend.
"she knows German, English, Spanish, and I don't
know how many other languages,"
Mats says of Stephanie admirably.
Stephanie and her friend walk up to give a happy hello,
reminding me of any gorgeously well-prepared
German girl who could knock the socks off of anyone
else around.
envious, yes, i was that,
of being able to speak so many different languages
and for
being so outgoing,
for i wished i could carry conversations with strangers
like her.
but envy aside, she drew me in and i was entranced.

the Camino is a mastermind.
let it weave its intricate web.

journal entry: April 11, 2022

Settled for the day,
i walked with my Swedes and we all decided to stop early
and rest
in a lovely town called Navarrete.
A delightful town with even more
delightful people.

This town is love.

We got here around 1pm.
Sat for a moment on our bunks after checking in with a
hospitalero who reminded me of the friendliest ranchero
mixed with
the charm and welcoming personality of my good friend
Chardmo,
fully dressed in a long beard, plaid flannel, and an
appetizing plan for dinner.
We were getting so hungry,
but first,
rest.
Rest and take off the boots.
Mend the toes,
check and re-wrap the blister,
then go out for some lunch.

We walked around after lunch and
What a beautiful town!
And the cathedral...
The Iglesia de Santa Maria de la Asunción,

took

my

breath

away.

i had to stop where i was and remind myself to breathe.
Tears came to my eyes, i felt so much.
An older Spanish lady approached me and said (en español),
"Santiago was here."
Chills.
i sat down in one of the pews and reflected for a while.
Overwhelmed by story,
by beauty,
by compassion,
by life's truths boiling to the surface.

i sit here now
with this journal in my lap and pen in hand and i think...
"i thought i'd have so much more time to write here."
Surprisingly
your time is filled with other moments and other people.
You're never truly alone,
there's always someone near,
up ahead,
just behind, or
walking alongside you.
It's nice to get to know so many people
from countries you've never known people before.
But times like these,
these quiet ones,
are also nice and very much needed.
It's in these moments, i can't help but think of home -
and life after this.

What will it look like?
Am i on the right road?

double-sided knife

the sun's asleep
the moon is out
faint snoring from across the room,
but it's not too bothersome.
i stare at the blue ceiling with yellow stars all around,
the sun is setting and night is coming.
i feel alone even though i'm surrounded by people.
the soft rustle of sleeping bags being adjusted.
the low mumble of a Danish man on the phone with his
family, (i'm guessing).
i place my earbuds in and push play,
my "Slow Dancing" playlist,
comfort music,
cry myself to sleep
after a heartwarming, intimate dinner with our host,
Mats, Monica, and a tall, thin, older Australian man
named Gary.
we all have stories to tell.
we all have spaces to hold.
we're all here for one another,
for one reason or another.

little do they know
they're each holding a gentle space for me,
to laugh and make light of,
to cry and grieve over,
to piece back together a life that quickly fell apart.
i wish i could tell them
how much i was hurting.
i wish they could hold my tears and reassure me
things would be okay.
i thought i was doing the right thing by staying quiet
about me and Paul.
but deep down
it felt like the opposite thing to do.
it felt like a double-sided knife that
no matter which way i turned,
no matter which dream i dreamt,

my soul was cut and my heart
was heavy.

this double-sided knife
of silencing my grief
is getting very hard to sleep with.

**only when it becomes more painful to stay silent,
do i begin to open up.**

day 10 - Navarrete to Azofra

lessons in leaving

i left Navarrete in tears
leaving behind Mats and Monica, as they take
a rest day.
i've found a home in them
i didn't expect.
a comforting duo that checked in on me,
texted when we weren't in the same village,
or called for wine when we were.
i liked knowing they were near,
like having a brother or a sister nearby
who understands
what you're going through.
and despite everything, they're there.

not knowing when i'd see them again,
it was hard to leave.
especially on this day
when i was missing Paul,
missing someone close,
a confidante,
an intimate partner to share all of life's ups and downs,
the Camino ups and downs,
the joys of seeing ducks for Dad
and the sorrows of grasping to memories as i tried to
fall asleep at night.

**at times i wished the Camino would erase memories
of lost loves,
for loss breaks me in two
and i'd like to be whole again.**

finding hearts

so many hearts along the Way today.
in rocks,
in puddles,
in tree lines,
in grassy patches.
a guiding love.

**i wonder if other people see them too...
or is it just me?**

and so, i walked on

i had planned on staying
in Nájera,
i picked out my albergue and
decided where i'd walk the next day
from there,
but i found myself
on a bench
at the edge of this little town
crying
from exhaustion
from hunger
from missing him who used to be
a fixed person in my life.
from missing Kym and the friend i could run to
with anything.
from the chaos that was the pandemic
and how it uprooted every part of my life
right down to
the very comfort of my home.
what was i doing?
why am i here?
and why don't i feel the warmth
in this town
that i've felt in so many others?

this town was not for me, i thought.
everything felt closed,
i would not stay here.
i could not give my slumber over
to a village that felt unwelcoming.
and to be honest,
i was not ready to stop.
i needed to walk.
if my body had allowed,
i would've walked all the way to Santiago...

and so, i walked on...

journal entry: April 12, 2022

Azofra.
i'm so glad i walked here and didn't stay in the town previous
as i had planned...

Nájera -
The vibe was all wrong for me.
Sitting on a bench at the edge of town
crying.
i needed another 5k to collect this heartache,
another dry, arid Spanish landscape to heal this pain,
to dry these tears and breathe some life in me again
into my lungs
into my heart
and burn life
back into my face.
i couldn't shake them
these chilly feelings,
i was hoping the warming temperatures would do so
as i rounded the corner from Nájera to wherever i was going
and found miles and miles of what reminded me of a South
African safari,
dry, hot, empty of green but full of life.
i walked and walked
until i reached Azofra.

The municipal albergue here in Azofra is one of the best.
Clean, cute, welcoming, and so helpful
for this Americana who knows very little about how to make
foreign washing machines work.
Only 10 euros for a bed in a 2-bed room that's immaculately
kept, charming in spirit
and a smile at the door with a helping heart.
i hardly slept last night.
Not for snoring
but for homesickness,
missing my kids
missing Paul

splitting from him hurts...
i feel heavy.
i realize what a shithead i was to him while he was here
and i'm sorry.
i should've snuggled with him more
i should've held his hand more
i should've kissed him more
i should've checked on him more
when he had stomach cramps -
What an ass i was!
Self-absorbed and wanting to be on my own.
i texted him all this and more,
which he appreciated
and gave me one of the biggest pep talks of my life.
And i wonder...
not that i'm thinking of giving up and going home
but

Why am i all the way over here, walking all this way
when all i feel is that i'm losing everyone i know?

day 11 - Azofra to Grañón

heaven and earth

"There are more things
in heaven and earth, Horatio,
than are dreamt of
in your philosophy."

– Shakespeare

i had the first line engraved in a ring for myself
with the second part in a ring for Kym.

my best friend -
whom i'd known since before my first marriage.
who'd seen every one of my babies just hours after they
were born.
whose back i leaned up against as we both got sick
from the night's overindulgence.
whose shoulders i climbed on in the darkest moments
of my life.
whose words talked me down from ledges.
who was always there
even when we didn't talk for months,
at one point, years.
she knew me and i knew her.

the news of her cancer's return
gutted me like the day's catch,
sliced and fried and served up for the closest carnivore.

someone so young shouldn't have to fight such a
dreadful illness.
though she fought it with valiant honor,
it ate her up like an infectious vine.

my soul sister.

i gave her that ring just weeks before she died.
we always loved that line from Shakespeare,
we said we'd get it tattooed together one day.

that day never came.

but the ring did
with the gracious etsy designer's engraved heart added
for love.
they said she held onto that ring
for hours on end,
sitting in her chair,
slouched in exhaustion but
looking at it with delight,
smiling so brightly,
"I love it so much"
rubbing it with her fingers
over and over again
holding it close,
"I'll take good care of it."

that was the last time i saw her.

it went missing,
my ring,
there in Azofra.
the same ring that took a deep dive down a bathroom
sink at Biscottis,
the same ring Chris, my manager, went after in that
bathroom sink because of his kind heart
(causing a visit from the plumber but finding my ring
in the process!)
she loved Biscottis...
maybe she wanted to hang out there for a while?
maybe some mozzarella bruschetta?
or mixed berry cake?
maybe she loved Azofra too...
i sure did. what a sweet little village.

i could see myself there again,
maybe she wanted to stay there for a while
or maybe she's telling me to
let go,
"i'm not ready yet, Kym. no, i'm not."
It's okay, I'm still here.

on the path between Azofra and Grañón
there was a sound of footsteps behind me,
mimicking my walk
but the pace
was in a different cadence than mine.
i saw a rock
in the shape of a heart
in a puddle beneath my feet.
i stopped to take a photo
and turned around,
no one was there.

was it you?

maybe it was you... i could use a friend.
thank you, Kym.

"I'll take good care of it!"

—

sometimes it's loud
and sometimes it's as soft as the petal of a flower.
but they're there,
our loved ones.
walking with us, guiding us, cheering us on
even when we think they aren't.

journal entry: April 13, 2022

i'm tired but good.
This blister on my pinky toe is growing
bubbling up and painful.
So much so, i've booked a hotel room for tomorrow night -
Tomorrow will be a rest day for me.
But tonight...
i'm staying in a donativo albergue
in a church tower!
So surreal
so cool
so amazing!
We each get two 1-inch mats to sleep on the hardwood floor,
but i gave one of mine to Mary, a sweet young German girl
i met walking today.

A fair-skinned, curly red-headed teenager
out here on her own.
We talked of my kids
and how inspiring she would be for them.
i would love for mine to be here,
walking and trying and trusting,
figuring it out as they go.

Mary was one of the last ones to get a spot
in this albergue tonight,
but there wasn't a mat for her.
i couldn't let her sleep on nothing
so i gave her one of mine.
not sure how much comfort a 1-inch plastic mat will
provide... but it's something.
i'm sitting on it now
and it's going to be a hard sleep for sure
but i'm happy.
Couldn't be happier to be sleeping in such a warm and
spiritual place.

Today, i walked mostly alone -

or so i thought...
Early this morning
as i walked through a long patch of tall grasses,
birds were chirping and singing
so melodically
that i nearly started singing with them.
i heard one particular bird start singing a tune
that sounded very much like something my youngest would
sing as a child,
skipping in a circle, round and round,
"peek-a-beek-a-beek-a-beek..."
it made me dizzy just watching
but they were so happy,
i didn't dare stop them.
i smiled thinking back.

Later, another bird chimed in with a cadence of sorts,
"left... left... left right left..." it sang.
Propelling me forward,
showing me love,
lifting my wings a little higher.

There were definitely spirits along the Way today.

the magic of Grañón

we were called down
from our thinly-supportive mats to help with dinner.
prep, cut, and prepare.
carrots, garlic, and potatoes
all as a community
getting to know one another
trying to communicate as best we could...
though most spoke English.
it was interesting learning where everyone was from
hearing their stories
telling mine
and feeling oddly comfortable
in the presence of strangers.

as dinner was cooking
in the oven of a nearby bakery,
we were led through a pilgrim's mass in the chapel of
Hospital de Peregrinos de San Juan Bauptista...
after mass, we were guided to the bakery
where we were asked to dance and sing for our dinner...
the Italians (of course) were the most animated,
they danced and sang their national anthem with such
heart and ecstasy that i was jealous i wasn't Italian,
the French did
what they do best -
win your heart over before singing the second note.
they sang La Vie En Rose
while the rest of us swayed
back and forth
dreaming of a love far away
wondering if they're thinking of us.
we Americans? ...grouped with the remaining
countries to sing
American Pie.
appropriate, right?
"the day the music died..."

our songs ended

with a chorus of "Let it Be" by the Beatles.
timely.
(i heard from friends
who didn't stay at this albergue
that we could be heard across town.
oh my heart.)

we danced and sang back to the church
only to find long tables end to end
with 30-35 chairs on either side
ready to seat us all for family dinner.
we crammed into this tiny room
but each had a space...
Germany, Holland, Italy, France,
Estonia, South Korea, USA, Denmark,
Hungary, Spain, and Australia.

when our bellies were full and our hearts complete,
we cleaned and dried the dishes and ourselves.
for that was a process i'd never seen,
getting all the remnants of dinner up
and out of the room
in record time...
a room where many would soon be relaxing and
settling in from the day.
for all 30 of us did it without question or hesitation,
even as tired as we were.

we were then invited to a meditation in the church -
10:00pm.
late, according to pilgrim daily bedtimes
and i so wanted to go to bed
but this i couldn't miss,
no, not this place,
a place where pilgrims have come to meditate for the
last thousands of years.
candles were lit
and old light fixtures were switched off.
the energy in the church was celestial.
this space,
overlooking the pews, the altar,

these wooden upright seats
joined together on all sides and connected at the edges
making a semicircle of prayer and energy.
we were given a personal candle to hold and light
and sit into the arms of our chairs.
we were then invited to pass one larger candle around
as we told our story,
what brought us here,
what we were here to let go of,
in our native language..
it didn't matter if our neighbor understood us or not,
we each spoke, one by one,
the words that would make us cry and unite in support.
strangers before we sat
but close friends after,
joining and giving hugs saying,
"i understand."

the longer i walk, the bigger the community grows.
the energy. the support.
the stories. the love.

new feelings

before the Camino,
my praying days had ended.

during the Camino,
my praying days (re)surfaced.

i've found a comfort in the church
that i've never experienced before.
is it the Way of St. James?
is it the gentleness of the Camino community?
is it me searching for something i've yet to feel?

whatever it is, i feel safe.

the Mind

"Somewhere between the start of the trail and the end of the trail is the mystery of why we choose to walk."

- unknown

day 12 - rest day in Grañón

finding my breath

miles from home and i couldn't feel closer.
the love i feel from
all around
cradles me like a newborn baby
with love and care,
concern and empathy.
i miss those i love at home
so much it hurts at times.
but i feel them with me
every step of the way.

i am carrying home
with me
and it doesn't feel so heavy.

threading the needle

the hotel was gracious and let me check-in at 9am
instead of the usual 3pm.
i showered, relaxed, facetime'd with Paul,
(it was lovely to see his face and talk for a while)
took a nap
then met Mats and Monica for a glass of wine
when i discovered they had made it to Grañón!

Monica told me about the needle and thread technique
for blisters...
something i had read about in my many hours of
research before starting out on this adventure
but was scared to try,
afraid of infection,
but she made it sound easy and simple,
"just clean it first," she advised.

so after washing my feet again and again
i sterilized the needle and thread that would be passing
through my skin,
(choosing a red thread to match Georgina and me)
gowned up like an episode of Grey's Anatomy
and started the procedure.
i was so proud of myself.
ready for the OR, right?
i giggled at my mini-cosplay.
squeezed as much liquid out of the blister as i could,
pressing tight with a gauze square and a clean towel,
spread a ribbon of triple antibiotic ointment on top
and wrapped it securely
in the ballet tape i used in college to prevent blisters in
the first place.

(boots or pointe shoes, they'll both eat your feet up
if you don't care for them properly.)

after my solo-operation,
i went down to grab a bite for dinner.

at My Way,
a bar nearby,
near the church and near my hotel,
playing from a tv tucked away in the corner of the bar
was Sting's Shape of My Heart...

oh my goodness,
oh my soul.

day 13 - Grañón to Villambistia

in the absence of

last night,
the hotel
was quiet.
almost too quiet.
a comfortable bed and room to myself,
i was surprised at how i was bothered by the quiet.
no snorers, i should be happy.
no one in my space, i should be elated.

it's funny the things we miss when they're not there.

tired

i'm beat.
the weather is turning very sunny
with little shade along the way.
thankfully it's not too hot
but i still sweat underneath my 20-pound pack
hiking throughout the day.
it felt heavier today than usual...
probably because i didn't wear it yesterday.
it's become a part of me
and i feel empty on days without it.

it felt good to get up and
walk again today.
i'm finding my rhythm,
my rhyme,
my flow.

they say the first week is for the body.
the second is for the mind.

if that's true,
go easy on me, Camino... for i have a lot to unwind.

the pull of Burgos

23km/14mi from Grañón to Villambistia
a very small town with only 1 albergue (12 beds).
i'm glad i called ahead,
i don't normally do that.
"the Camino provides"
is what i live by.
but tonight, i'm glad i did.
this one is full
and i know i wouldn't have found space
'til the next town,
which i did not have the energy for.
Mats and Monica stopped in Belorado,
but i wanted to go a bit further.
my goal is to make it to Burgos for Easter Sunday…
so many of my friends will be there.

the city is calling me.

volume in the silence

12 beds, 6 bunk beds, above a bar.
the only albergue in town.
and i was wise to call ahead
(something i hardly ever do)
because it was full
but oh so sweet.

our host made us a dinner of fresh salad, pasta with
mussels in an olive oil sauce, bread, wine (4 bottles!),
then ice cream for dessert.
so good.

this American sat next to a handful of Germans,
including Moritz -
a twenty-something handsome guy
who beamed sincere charm
and the intelligence of an old soul.
we chatted like classmates on the first day of school.
"what do you do? where are you from?"
the conversation felt nice and easy, as the rectangular
table filled with the rest of the albergue residents for
the evening.
two Italian girls, a couple of native Spaniards
each walking their own portion of the Camino,
"one week here,
another two weeks there..."
and an elderly lady from Finland who came in quiet,
head down,
and sat at the end of the table,
only greeting us with a slight nod and a gentle
side-eye.
i didn't get her name. i don't think anyone did,
for she didn't speak.
at first, i thought she was sad (and maybe she was)
but i believe it's because she didn't speak any of the
languages around her,
only Finnish,
and none of us spoke hers.

i can't imagine how alienating that must've felt.
i tried to offer more water and wine
but got brushed off.
i didn't take it personally - I know how it is.
i've certainly had my days of wanting to be left alone.

after dessert,
when the bottles of wine were empty
and the hostess gathered all the plates and flatware,
the Finnish woman rose from the table to go upstairs.
if her spiritual or emotional struggle was hidden,
her physical one was certainly evident.
she walked hunched over at the waist,
unable to stand upright.
i looked around the table and saw humility on all of our
faces...
she's walking the Camino like that?
we have NOTHING to complain about.

the volume of the silence filled the room.

i went to bed thinking...
had i had more time with these lovely people at dinner,
been able to communicate better,
we would've become greater friends.

great people with great stories.
great people with enormous hearts.

**sometimes you hear more in the silence
than in a room full of noise.**

day 14 - Villambistia to Atapuerca

tucking in for the night

what a gorgeous sunrise
over Villambistia this morning
as i looked back on the village.
on my way to Atapuerca.
and i heard my first cuckoo bird in the wild!
for so long i thought they existed only in clocks.

today's hike was long and tiring
with a long stretch of 11km/7mi
and nothing in between
but red dirt, trees,
and a pilgrim stop with juices and fruits.
i made it though.
23 kilometers/14 miles and i'm here in Atapuerca.
with CANADA!!

everyone seems to be stopping in Burgos tomorrow.
as am i.
there should be a lot of reunions,
so sweet to think of.

going to sleep before the sun,
as i do most nights now.
crazy, huh?

goodnight.

wait... what?!

not so fast!
no sleep yet...

ENTER Heidi.

a German girl who arrived late and was assigned to
the third bed in our room.

(Jacey and i were quietly reading and prepping for
tomorrow's walk,
we did not expect this burst of laughter and light
to come blazing through the dark!)

she tells us she took a
wrong turn
and ended up walking 40km (25mi)!
(what the hell, girl?!)
i felt bad for her but then again i would've just stopped
somewhere else
and found a bed...
she said she came across "some Spanish man"
(her words)
who brought her here to Atapuerca.
she unbuckled her pack,
slung it down to the floor and
proceeded to tell us how hot she was.
she took off every article of clothing
right down to her underwear
bent over to get her water bottle from the pocket
in her pack and stood up
with all her nakedness out for us to see.
no shame.
no modesty.
just her big, beautiful, natural breasts and tight ass
in sight,
...not a blemish or stretch mark to speak of.
(i don't know about Jacey, but i was jealous)
and she was SO dramatic,

but in the best way possible.
it was hard to keep a straight face...
much less, keep my eyes in my book.
we laughed
and nodded along with the story,
then she left to shower.
thank God.

now can i get some sleep please?

day 15 - Atapuerca to Burgos

easter sunday with angels

i knew i wanted to make it to Burgos by noon
for Easter Sunday,
but i was starting in Atapuerca
and i knew i had a steep climb ahead of me.
i also knew i hadn't eaten anything this morning
and that would slow me down.
no breakfast offered at the albergue
and nothing open in this town yet.
too early.
so i grabbed the last of the cookies i had in my pack
and started on.
Jacey stayed back to catch up with a friend.

the climb over the mountains was steep and rocky.
full of boulders, big and small.
nowhere could i put my foot and not feel uprooted
by stone or gravel.
the descent down into the valley was no more
forgiving.
it took every ounce of concentration
and careful foot placement
not to slip
and hurt something.
but
i had to get to Burgos.

i had to record the church bells for my mom.
one of her absolute favorites!
especially on this day.
(i had no idea i'd have the chance to send her something
even better.)

almost 7km/4.5mi in and i reached a town with
un café abierto con desayuno!
"...una tortilla con chorizo, napolitana de chocolate y

café con leche, por favor,"
was becoming an easy phrase to repeat
over and over again with delight.
it all went down easy and fast,
deliciously,
amongst friends outside in a green valley
cradled quietly in a circle of mountains
with red plastic tables and chairs.
the valley of Cardeñuela Ríopico,
exactly what i needed to make it to Burgos,
another 14km to go.

it didn't take long for my post-breakfast walk towards
Burgos to turn from
a luscious, green countryside to a
12km/7.5mi walk through highways,
construction sites,
and city streets.
i had heard of an alternative route
along the river,
but either i missed the signs
or they had been taken down.
(i'd heard of this happening, for some locals want to
(re)direct pilgrims to certain routes)
i saw no way to the "River Route" into Burgos.
but it didn't matter,
even though my feet were aching from the
over-abundance of concrete beneath my boots,
i'm glad i didn't find the alternate route.
for had i found it,
i wouldn't have come across three more Angels of the
Camino on this day.

the first,
a nice man who stopped me along a busy highway
to chat,
crossing paths on a sidewalk at an overpass,
in a combination of Spanish and English
reassuring me
"it's not a pretty walk, but it's only 10km (6mi) more."

the second,
a lovely older couple
walking hand-in-hand
in the opposite direction as me
gave big smiles,
a pat on my back,
and the warmest "¡buen Camino!"
no other words were needed.
their sincerity hit deep.

the third,
a man from Slovakia,
a driver of one of the hundreds of semi-trucks
lining the 4-lane highway into Burgos.
he spoke no English,
and i spoke not a word of his language.
how we were able to hold a small, meaningful
conversation is
beyond me.
beyond words.

receiving reassurance from locals
who know pilgrims
and of their struggles and plight
is a comfort that is hard to explain...
i've tried to equate it to something back home
but i keep coming up empty.

there is an energy here
that everyone rides,
willingly or not,
it keeps us going with smiles in tough times and
tears when needed to wash away the pain.
we're all here together,
peregrino o no.

**we're all here walking the same path,
whether to Santiago or back home,
whether to work or to see a friend...
we're all walking the same.**

burgos

i reached the city limit of Burgos
looked at my map and saw i had
three and a half kilometers
(2 more miles!)
to the Plaza Mayor.
how could this be?
i did not expect this ciudad grandioso to be so
expansive.

over on a bench
resting before taking the long walk into Burgos
was Moritz.
a familiar face!
his young, German charm beamed back,
"a sight for sore eyes! how are you?!" i asked.
"not so good," he said through a sad smile, "i shouldn't
have bought brand new boots right before coming."
he told me of all the blisters that were forming
on his feet.
i had read many warnings of this.
i was so sad for him.
he wasn't sure he'd make it
and was waiting for a friend to catch up to help.
i wanted to help but how?
the only thing i could do was call a taxi
or just sit with him for a while.
i chose the latter
since a friend had already done the former.
just for comfort
i was there.
just a little "i got you, you're doing okay," until he
figured out his next move.

new boots are the death of a pilgrim.
break those babies in, my friend.
break 'em in hard
is what i read prior to coming here.
and i'm glad i listened.

for later on, i learned Moritz had to go home.
his 30+ blisters stopped his physical Camino while the
rest of us carried on.
again, my heart ached for him.

i crossed the river and walked towards the city center
and was greeted with the reason for its expansiveness...
the colors that brought this city to life,
the laughter
the conversation
the people,
family and friends alike,
food and wine
markets and shops
so much contained in this small part of the city,
no wonder
its borders had to expand.

squeezing into the packed streets
lined with celebration and grandeur
i walked right into an Easter procession so lively
it put anything i've ever seen of its size in America to
shame.
the music
the clapping
the singing
the celebration
the spirit
the colors
the rustic
unpolished and unprocessed
realness and authenticity.
it all passed by with such strength, grace, confidence,
and vitality that
i just stepped aside
against a stone wall of a restaurant or shop
(of which i was unsure)
and took it all in,
watching in awe
the smiles on their faces,
from the young, unable to walk on their own two feet

to the elderly being guided by hand or in wheelchairs.
i pulled out my camera and knew i was being touristy
but didn't care.
i could not let this moment go by without capturing it
forever.

i only hoped i was capturing the joy in their hearts too.

when the procession passed,
i made my way towards the Cathedral Plaza
expecting to meet some friends...
instead
i was met by the vastly climbing cathedral steeples
reaching higher and higher into the sky
than the birds themselves.

stopping and staring,
my eyes did their best to take it all in.
every detail,
every stone,
every carving,
every point,
every curve
every chisel mark,
each bolder that was a wonder in how it even got there.

suddenly a chorus singing Handel's Halleluia came
through the air
to surround me.
(one of my mom's favorites!)
it penetrated every nook and cranny of this enchanted
town until you could feel the gloriousness bounce off
the square.

this was the most joyous day.
perhaps the most joyous Easter Sunday i'd witnessed
in all of my 45 years.

journal entry: April 17, 2022

Easter Sunday
and i made it to Burgos
just in time to see processions and hear the bells.
Amazing.
i've never really been one to celebrate Easter -
except to make baskets packed with stuffed animals
and chocolates
for my kids when they were young.
Honestly, it's one of my least favorite holidays back home,
but here, it's different.
Easter here in Spain feels so very special,
Spiritual.
Motherly.
Nurturing.

i'm staying in a very nice hotel
right above the plaza and the cathedral
with two of my dearest friends on the Camino,
Bekah and Suzanne.
My Gregory pack buds and fellow Americans i met in Zubiri.
They were so sweet to offer me the extra bed in their room
when they discovered they had one.
So nice of them.
And the shower! Oh my word, the shower,
the water pressure!
Heaven.
Even the shampoo and conditioner bottles offered words of
encouragement...

"Have a nice day...
(Que tengas un bien día)"
"You are wonderful...
(Tú eres maravilloso)"
"Never give up...
(Nunca te rindas)"
and
"Keep your smile every day...

(Manten tú sonrisa cada día)"
read the labels.

(The things we take for granted.)

My legs are sore but today was a good day.
i'm amazed at how i walk 22km/13mi so easily now
(well... relatively)
Some days are shorter, some days are longer,

whatever your body is needing and your spirit is craving,
lean in and listen.

binds

do you ever wonder what holds people together?

what
keeps some
from falling apart

while others break
at the first blustery wind?

any longer

all of my friends and family
watched me fall down
and when i surfaced to breathe
it was all under me, my town.
my world, my everything
you had so easily become,
but so quickly, perhaps overnight?
you and i were no longer one.

everyone thought i had
the world at my fingertips.
traveling here and there with
annual vacations and elaborate trips.
they said my three kids
finally had a dad now,
but you didn't want to be bothered,
only when you decided to be around.

you blamed the alcohol on us
and your increased responsibilities.
you made me feel i wasn't good enough,
such high expectations to please,
we could never get close enough
my family, my kids, or me.
were we just a cross off your list?
a trial-run to see what could be?

i put all my trust in you
and in all the words you said.
i trusted this life and our path
we signed up to tread.
no where in my heart of hearts
did i ever think you'd regress
and turn this into a storm,
a mangled, torn-up mess.

our world came tumbling down
for your selfish desire to be alone.

my world came tumbling down
my kids and me, all on our own.
for the third time you chose
to live a life without us there,
for the third time you chose
we were just too much to bear.

i believed this time was the one,
for you had come back again,
but me, i was the foolish girl
to believe your fears you'd mend.
i once felt sorry for you,
for you too have deeply hidden scars.
but you refused to see it takes two...
you can't heal hearts from afar.

broken and ashamed, i'm here
with all of my deepest grief,
realizing life is much better when
you don't have to swim so deep.
the currents are strong and
the undertow even stronger,
but with you i was drowning
with you i couldn't breathe any longer.

day 16 - Burgos to Arroyo San Bol

the meseta

that long stretch
between Burgos and León,
bus or taxi,
a lot of people withdraw.
"nothing to look at,"
they so often say.
that redundant stretch of silence and
reflection that goes on for days...
time to think
time to remember
time to sift through
time to sever
time to awaken
all that has brought you here.
to many who have come,
this Way brings aches and tears.
but if you let it, the Meseta
will trace your scars and smooth your fears.
"bear them to me without fear, my friend."
i dried my eyes and was jarred
out of my body and into my head.

the Meseta takes its toll
on your mind and your soul.
it opens your heart and prompts you to think
of why you're here and what brought you to your brink.
from dissolution and despair
you begin to heal your heart's deepest tear.
you're walking all this way on your own...
you doubt your strength and yet you know
that you have splintered, yes this is true
but you'll mend your broken pieces with golden glue.

journal entry: April 18, 2022

i am officially within
the Meseta -
green fields all around
for miles and miles
blanketed in every direction
with blue skies.
And the WIND!
My goodness, the wind.
A constant blowing from one end of forever to the next
like its very existence depended on it.
At one point in my hike today,
the wind was blowing so hard...
i stopped in the middle of the dirt road,
turned around,
a complete
slow
circle
around,
not another person nearby,
but i could see the wind
flying by
on both sides.

Have you ever SEEN the wind?

i thought at first i was hallucinating
(perhaps i was, for exhaustion sets in quickly under this sun)
but i knew i wasn't.
It was as real as the blades of grass leaning
in their submission.

The Meseta...
i had done my research
prior to arriving.
The Meseta made me nervous,
in all honesty.
Would i be able to walk its lengthy path?

Would i be able to quiet the endless mind chatter?
All the inner noise that this time would open up and bring
to the forefront?
Even one hospitalero in Grañón said, "I'm starting in León.
The Meseta scares me."

Its expansiveness works its way into your psyche,
into your bones.
But its magic will take you over
'til you're under its spell.
A universal space
where all thoughts are welcome
without judgement,
just ultimate care.
Here, the Camino welcomes emotion,
for its winds are seeking validation themselves -
in you, from you, for you,
a symbiotic union.
They whip and wind around your soul
circling you from root to crown,
opening the margins to pull your pieces back together.

It is everything i'd read about and more,
this Meseta.

i'm glad i didn't take a taxi - i'm glad i placed each foot
in front of the other and
walked it.
Honoring it.
Trusting it.
Guided by it.

My albergue tonight is absolutely amazing.
Beautiful.
Calm.
Quiet.
With music.
i've showered and the hospitalero has washed my clothes
and i hung them out to dry,
clipping each piece tight with clothes pins
(hoping and praying they don't blow away in this WIND).

The hospitalera is in the kitchen
cooking dinner
(the scents and the sounds, intoxicating)
Only 3 of us peregrinas tonight,
Helma from Holland, Kerstin from Germany, and me,
within a very sturdy place to be,
the wind roaring outside
like a hoard of bees seeking the perfect flower.
Not one inch of this place moves
in this earth-shattering Meseta wind
beyond its walls.
i'm amazed i don't feel a thing in here ...

Last night in Burgos,
i had dinner with Mats and Monica, Bekah and Suzanne,
and it brought my spirits up a bit.
i was a little down.
Missing family and home
ending things with Paul
yet knowing he wants to keep in contact,
it's confusing to me.
i'm sure we'll remain friends, right?
i'm (trying) learning to let go and trust.
It's impossible to know what's going to happen next.
i'm not supposed to know, right? No one is,
not today
not tomorrow
not a year from now
not ever.

Trust in myself
trust in the process
trust in the Universe
and know everything will be okay.

Control is an illusion,
and knowing the future is a luxury not even the wind has.

day 17 - Arroyo San Bol to Itero de la Vega

journal entry: April 19, 2022

Today was tough.
4 degrees Celsius/40 degrees Fahrenheit
all day
with iron-handed wind,
drizzling rain,
and a huge hill to climb
with my poncho trying to swallow me whole
coming up from the bottom to around my head.
At one point, i was so angry with the wind
because it seemed to want to fight back,
it picked up in velocity and force
just to spite.
That's when i rolled my eyes,
threw my gripped hands up in the air and said,
*"f*ck it!"*
and just kept walking.
Drenched or not.
What else was i to do?

i walked alone today
again
except for a kind man from Wales
who was rushing to catch up with his sister.
We chatted for a bit
then he was off and over the hill,
but not before advising,
"What's goes up, must always come back down."

His disappearance
reminded me of a line from The Wizard of Oz...
"People come and go so quickly around here."
(It's strange what references come to mind while walking)

With all the wind and rain and being tossed about
i was weary and tired and thought

"Wouldn't a private room be nice right now?"
But i didn't want to pay hotel prices tonight.
So i walked to an albergue that sounded nice
(after checking on one that had no heat...
wet and cold from the day? NO THANK YOU)
and
much to my surprise
she gave me a private room,
a twin bed, not hotel comfortable, but i'll take it!
i was so grateful.
Shared bath, but that's ok.

There are only two other pilgrims here -
two Italian men.
Quiet, reserved. Unusual for Italians, and that's okay too.
Again, i welcomed the calm.
And the bath,
it's the biggest private bath i've seen anywhere on the
Camino yet!
i must've spent 15 minutes in the shower
spraying myself with hot water,
minute after long minute
letting the warmth swallow me down to the bone.
After rainy, frigid weather all day long, it felt amazing.
i didn't care if the other pilgrims needed the bath.
i needed this hot water
in this moment.

And i needed food.
They don't cook for you here but at least there's a
supermercado just beneath me
and a kitchen downstairs.

i've been thinking about what i want to do when i get back.
This town and the one before (Castrojeriz)
are super cute.
As i walked down the streets,
noticing all the "for sale" signs,
i fantasized about buying one
to live and write
and perhaps run as an albergue

part of the time.

i don't know,
i have a whole month before going back.
Lots of time to think.

day 18 - Itero de la Vega to Villarmentero de Campos

journal entry: April 20, 2022

The past 2 days i've been walking alone.
i've needed the time to think
time to feel my body
the walking
the aches
the pains
the endorphins
the peace
the wind
the rain
the sun
and the silence.

The wind was so brutal today, again, that
i was completely worn-out after 23km/14mi.
i chose a hotel
warm with dark wood and stone,
fire going in the hearth downstairs
a comfortable bed in my room adjacent to an open window
with views to write home about.
i had my own room and own bathroom,
i could shower and not worry if someone else needed it,
i could walk around naked if i chose or play music to my
heart's content.

i must be the only pilgrim in the hotel though
for i was the only one at dinner, a pilgrim's dinner
complete with 3 courses and a bottle of wine.
As i ate, i watched a flock of sheep be herded around the
field and thought
"it'd be nice to share this with someone right now..."

Tomorrow i'll see friends in Carrión.
It's a short walk to Carrión,

only 10km/6mi
but following Carrión is a long stretch
with nothing in between,
17km/10mi
no water, no shelter from the sun, wind, or rain.
Whatever we're given from the heavens is what we have
to walk through.
So probably best not to end my day with that,
save it for the next morning when i'm rested.

lose your way

*lose your way
and i will follow.
wander the plains
and feel your sorrows.
cry out a tear
for what enslaves your heart,
lean into the fear
of forever being apart.*

you're not the one
who gave it all up
beneath the sun
and into a rut,
drinking whiskey
and red wine,
when lies and honesty,
deciphering, had no time.

your brokenness
will mend
amongst kindness
that is heaven-sent,
amongst people
new and old,
those pilgrims
who share your soul.

trust in yourself
and all you can do.
trust in yourself,
in all that is true.
find a face
within the shadows,
spirited with grace
and wildflower meadows,

alive with hope
and vivid dreams

that soon you'll sow
into all the seams.
*you'll find your way
and i will still follow;
until the end of days,
my strength you can borrow.*

day 19 - Villarmentero de Campos to Carrión de los Condes

journal entry: April 21, 2022

i'm in Carrión de los Condes.
Following two days of long hikes
offensive winds
and cold temps,
an easy day into this lovely town was nice.

And wow, is this village alive!

Thursday is Market Day
and there are people everywhere.

i decided to stay in one of the monasteries here,
Santa Maria,
i was craving people.
The nuns are SO nice.
They offered me a hot tea and piece of chocolate
when i walked in,
one even carried my pack upstairs to my bed for me.
They don't offer dinner or breakfast
but there's a supermarket nearby,
i need snacks anyway.
Hopefully Mats and Monica will make it to town for dinner.

i'm sitting in one of the plazas
having just had lunch
and writing
with a glass of wine (of course)
and the sun shining down brightly on my journal.
What could be better?

i'm here walking this Way alone
with many around me,
and it makes me realize
i'm not supposed to be doing this alone.

We're a community of seekers and lovers
dreamers and visionaries
who sometimes want tiny bits of comfort
and the validation only a kindred spirit could offer.
Is that so wrong?
i don't think it is.
But i'm happy to be doing this on my own,
it's giving me such strength and hope
knowing i'll be fine.

...but
can i share this with you?
My friends, near and far and online,
our connection,
it's a distant connection, this i know
where i get to choose how close each friend gets,
because in the end
i'm scared.
i know this about myself.
That protective skin i weave around my heart.
i don't like that i do it
but i do.
My brain says, "Protect your heart.
Protect your energy."

What if i love with abandon? What then?
Would i still break as hard in the end?

journal entry: same day, later in the evening

i just returned from a nice time with Mats and Monica in
the Plaza Mayor here in Carrión.
We had a glass of wine,
Skål! ("cheers" in Swedish),
some dinner,
then stopped in the supermercado for our breakfast and
lunch tomorrow.
i'm glad we all ended up here tonight.
My Gregory pack friends, Bekah and Suzanne, are here too,
though i didn't see them.
i heard from them by WhatsApp -
they're staying at the church up the road.
Another monastery.
i'm guessing a lot of people stopped here
before the long, hard walk tomorrow.

Now off to get some sleep.
i didn't sleep very well last night at all.
Perhaps too quiet?
Funny, huh?

day 20 - Carrión de los Condes to Terradillos de Los Templarios

bye, beautiful Carrión

bye, beautiful town,
Carrión de los Condes,
your people, your spirit, your love for peregrinos...
thank you.

but first, a new poncho!
it's raining again and
i wasn't going to take
another miserably failed Marilyn Monroe attempt
today.
(a friend said, "at least you can laugh at yourself."
yes, **now** i can. back there, when the wind was crazy,
i couldn't.)

No no...
thankfully there was a shop open
bright and early this morning
for this pilgrim in need
with the perfect poncho -
full, long sleeves,
covers me AND my pack,
and reaches all the way down to my calves
in the front AND the back.

muy bien. ¡muchas gracias!
i handed over my awful,
(Amazon said it was the best?)
green, poor-excuse of a poncho
with gusto
to the nice gentleman behind the counter saying,
"do what you wish with it. ¡muchas gracias!"

he smiled, ¡buen Camino!

journal entry: April 22, 2022

i'm settled in my albergue for the night.
Rooming with a girl from South Korea, Choi,
who's got a smile that brightens the darkest room,
and Olga, an older lady from Germany
who frustrated me a bit when she hung her wet clothes
over a clothesline
she stretched from my opposing bunkbed corner
to hers,
blocking my way out except for
underneath her dripping poncho.

Ugh.

i showered, gave my clothes over for a washing
(worn 2 days in a row,
no shower last night,
slept in them -
i think they deserve a good washing.)

Now i'm sitting at the bar in the albergue
next to a fire
with a glass of wine and writing.
Trying to ward off some guy in his 20s
who insists on having a conversation with me,
even though i'm pen in hand, face to paper, clearly
concentrating on
anything but him -
kudos to him for persistence but a little space would be nice.
Asking my age and professional history and saying,
"i need to have my eyes checked because right now, they're
deceiving me."
Seriously?
Sometimes i wish i had a sign,
"Don't hit on me. i'm not interested."
Not to sound ungrateful but really, that's not why i came.
i hear this from a few other girls too...
We're not here to find love, or lust even. So please, thank you
but no thank you.

Nevo,
was his name.
He asked mine and,
which is quite typical for anyone hearing my name
for the first time,
he asked me to repeat it
then pulled out his notebook and pen and asked me to
write it out,
showing me his journal entries
i couldn't read at all, for they were in Hebrew
written from right to left.
He even pointed that out, "See, we write this way."
It was very interesting to see
and i told him so.

i went back to writing
and he returned to his book to write too.

Choi soon joined our circle next to the fire
with her own glass of wine and journal to write.

Today was tough.
17km/10mi at the start with nowhere to stop.
wind. rain. cold. hail even
at one point...
HAIL?!
We laughed at it saying, "is this real?!"

All of us
head down,
focused on the road,
straight ahead,
ready for our next stop
already,
after only a few steps into the driving rain.
There was so much rain that even the snails were climbing
out of the ditch and onto the road, trying to find dry land.
i thought we'd never reach Calzadilla.
Every hope on the horizon
turned out to be a farmhouse

or a cloud.
And my hands were too cold to
reach into my pocket for my phone
to check the map,
so foot in front of the other foot, i continued.

Somewhere between
the big snail crossing and the faux towns of barnyards
i had to go to the bathroom.
But there was no toilet to be found.
i told Suzanne and she offered to block me if we found a dip
in the road for privacy.
So... on the side of a tiny bridge crossing a quiet stream
pinging with raindrops,
i walked down,
hiked my backpack high on my back,
pulled up my poncho and lowered to the ground,
as conspicuously as i could
thinking...
Man, guys have it so much easer!

With everything back in place
though a little more damp from the rain than before,
i finally saw what could be a town
again
up ahead.
i thought to myself, "Don't get your hopes up, Sabrie.
Could be just another farmhouse..."
But it wasn't.

It was Calzadilla, with warm tortillas and hot coffee!

Everyone stopped here.
Everyone rushed for a seat inside the tiny café.
Those who didn't get a seat inside bore the brunt of the
weather beneath a covered patio within the courtyard.
Fortunately for me,
my can do! friends, Bekah and Suzanne
grabbed a table with chairs inside
and we warmed the freeze off of our souls.

i started out this morning with Mats and Monica,
but my pace was a little faster than theirs
and they wanted to hang back a little, so
Suzanne and i walked and talked
nearly the whole way to Calzadilla.
It was nice having someone to talk to
to take your mind off the rain and cold
to make the 17 kilometers go by a little faster.

i had lunch with Bekah and Suzanne before continuing
on my way
after seeing Mats and Monica checking into their albergue
for the night.
i know i'll see them again.
and i know i'll see Suzanne again
somewhere up the road,
but Bekah...
her Camino journey is soon coming to an end.
She'll be turning towards Madrid tomorrow
to catch a flight to Cairo
where the rest of her sabbatical continues.
i gave her a big hug, an even bigger "Buen Camino", and
wished her safe travels.
May you always take extra butter with your toast!

i walked on after lunch
in the rain
alone
not knowing if i'd stop at the next village or the one after.
But a larger group came up behind me
into the first town with available albergues
and helped me with that decision...
they were so loud that i knew
i wanted to be anywhere but there.
So i kept walking
to Terradillos de Los Templarios.

i like this trusting in the moment and trusting myself.
Knowing what i want and continuing until i get there.

halfway

i am officially halfway to Santiago.
feels good.
there's been a lot of time to think,
thoughts pop in and out and i work through them,
giving myself pep talks along the way
to carry on,
step by step.
carry on, wayward son
...one of Kym's favorite songs
plays in my head.

day 21 - Terradillos de Los Templarios to Bercianos del Real Camino

a ray of light

> "Good morning Sabrie. Today is the day! Gonna take a drive up to see you. Please let me know which town you'll be stopping at for the afternoon/night and we can have tapas or something. So excited to finally meet with you in person!!"

(from my dear friend, Jane)

today's ray of light.

the first day is the hardest?

today was completely awful.
you could say it rivaled
my first day on the Camino
with the most brutal winds
to walk against
at an angle
so i wouldn't blow over.
cold
rainy
unbearable
puddle after puddle
head down
forcing myself
through the wind
and the rain.
and what made it ten times worse
is that some of the yellow arrows
showing the Way
were painted over
and i lost my way.
backtracking through streets and highways
my tears matched the raindrops
pouring over me.
i think i cried more today
than on any other day so far.
extremely hard.
an unforgivingly emotional day.
i wanted home.
i wanted warmth.
i wanted rest.
i wanted to be held
but by who
now?
i wanted the weather to let up and
not be so hard to walk through.
i was tired.
i was so tired,
and the tears kept coming

so hard
like this day
falling down
with force and persistence
challenging the unforgiving storm that let loose
on my way today.

hearts everywhere

the hearts kept me going.
head down
into the wind
and rain.

hearts everywhere -

there is love here,
this, i know,
right here.
there is love.

soul friends

Jane and her partner, Quino, came to meet me
in Bercianos del Real Camino.
not only were they a pair of shining faces
to brighten my dreariest of days
but they soothed over my hospitalera
by speaking fluent Spanish and helping me
communicate a few things.
maybe the cold, rainy weather was getting to her also
for she seemed to have had enough
of the oncoming peregrinos
and their varied ways.

Jane is a special soul who i met on instagram
through a mutual love of Thula Thula (an animal refuge
in South Africa)
and its elephants.
(sometimes social media does amazing things)
a spunky, short-haired Brit living in Spain with
Quino, a native of Madrid and artist whose mind rivals
that of Picasso's.

we walked and walked in search of wine,
down quiet streets of boarded up businesses and
homes
to find the only open bar in Bercianos del Real Camino,
and it was packed.
loud and Spanish and lovely.
"the louder, the better, here in Spain," Jane said
smiling. "isn't it wonderful?"
they bought me a pizza and gave me a little gift bag,
"i didn't want to bring anything too big, because i know
you have to carry it," Jane said.
with an inspirational book, chocolate, a friendship
bracelet, and a few more candies, she warmed my heart
and soul on this very cold and sad day.
such love and care.
we enjoyed multiple glasses of wine,
smiling each time we asked for another

and talked for over three hours
like talking to an old friend.

i know we just met
but i'm certain we'll be friends
until Time has no more time to give.

day 22 - Bercianos del Real Camino to Mansilla de las Mulas

journal entry: April 24, 2022

Today's weather was much better.
Still cold in the morning (2 Celsius/36 Fahrenheit)
but calm with clearer skies.
The sun came out to join the walk
after the morning grew to life,
it was a beautiful day.
The energy on the Camino was much different too,
much happier than the last two days.

kundalini, possibly?

something happened today while walking
that has never happened to me before...
was it the energy of the Camino? or
was it something else?

... i was into my hike,
into my mind, into the surroundings,
all alone.
there were pilgrims way up ahead
and pilgrims far, far behind,
no footsteps or lingering conversations carried
on the breeze,
no walking sticks hitting the ground heard with ease.
i was into my body, into the
trees lining my way and
the snow-capped mountains off in the distance,
the new life of spring smiling in the sun,
grasses bending in the wind circling me,
i felt warm and sensual,
every cell in my body amplified, feeling the movement
of my feet on the ground and my pack on my back,
in the rhythm of my legs moving back and forth
in opposition to my arms
back and forth, back and forth,
my mind went to him
to pleasuring him and
him pleasuring me.
my mouth around his body
making him so hard that my lips began to swell
with excitement,
my breasts sharpened from my chest
and my shortened breath steepened in quickness...
i felt him inside me
enlarged and full
acquiring every space
so warm and sure,
in and out, in and out,
i let go of all control

in and out
in and out,
what happened was all i know
right there,
while walking,
one foot in obedience to the other.
no sound,
complete stillness
except my eruption inside.
the sun became brighter
and my senses came alive.
i found my breath and my vision returned
remembering where i was...
comforted
and safe.
felt
and heard.

it was the most sensual,
most erotic thing
i have ever experienced
on my own.

can something so erotic be spiritual at the same time?
i am starting to believe so.
but this wasn't about him.
this was about me
and my (re)gaining of confidence.
this, i know so far.

but what was this? "this" that just happened,
this energy that surged through my body
as a lightning bolt surges through the sky...
my old self twisting and weaving into my new self?
or my old self dying and giving birth
to my new self?
this, i wondered so far...

it is said that...

"Significant life experiences impact us with energy at high voltage, a level that our physical, emotional and intellectual selves are not prepared to handle." — from Returning From Camino by Alexander John Shaia

i thought i had just been handed
all of the answers
to all of my questions
right then and there
on the Camino
between Bercianos del Real Camino and
Mansilla de las Mulas,
but what really had been given to me
was a new source of energy -

this, i researched and read and found to be true.

this fire
and bolt of life
was new to me
for it came in a wave i'd never felt before.

sure, i know of the energy one experiences during a
"good" yoga session...
that feeling of deep zen, of pure bliss
and being a yoga practitioner and teacher,
i'm aware of kundalini -
an energy believed to rest coiled at the base of the spine
with potential to rise, and
when this energy does rise,
it travels up from the sacrum
through all seven chakras
to the crown of the head,
the highest chakra,
and is set free.

when kundalini energy is released,
there are associated feelings and emotions

from elation and euphoria to deep stillness and peace,
even sadness and tears too, depending on your life
at the moment.

but in my moment,
i wasn't sure what this energy and sensation was...

was it kundalini or something else?
had i just tapped into the energy of the Camino
or was it something even bigger?
this energy that traveled back and forth
in waves and rhythms,
in pulses and heartbeats,
from the positive to the negative
and back again,
until it formed a figure eight
with oscillations varying in strength and intensity.

i was trying to organize it
in my mind,
i was trying to understand it
in my mind,
i found myself rationalizing
everything and nothing,
somewhere and something
that couldn't be rationalized,
in my mind.

only in my heart
and within my soul.

i knew i needed to allow "it" space.
i knew i needed to allow "it" growth,
this energy
that engulfed every peak and valley of my being.
i knew i needed to be present and let go of control
but it's hard when you've stepped into
an unknown realm.
we rush to name it, we rush to claim it.
was this euphoria?
was this peace?

was this my peace?
is this my undoing?
this is me,

just let it be.

when it happened, it was difficult to believe it was anything other
than what it seemed on the surface.
but as time went on, the pieces of me that i found and glued together
told a different story.

it is said that
this can happen anywhere along your path...
as you walk,
at your turn-around,
on your way home,
or even after you've been home for a while.

"This energy is actually helping you experience the intellectual and emotional chasm between the vitality in your new sense of self and the lack of energy in your "old" self. You feel a growing intense dissonance between who you have been, and who you are in the process of becoming." —
from Returning From Camino by Alexander John Shaia

welcome to you, my friend.
don't be afraid.
dive in.

shallow

i was starving and ate a pilgrim's meal early.
i tried to hold out as long as i could,
to go downstairs into the bar and order at a more
typical dinner time
but
my stomach won.
5pm and i was eating,
back upstairs by 6pm
when everyone else was heading down
to eat.

i didn't mind though.
this albergue had 40 beds in two rooms.
so as they all headed out to eat,
i settled in to write,
showered and stomach full.

only 3 other pilgrims remained in the room.
two girls, one with a gorgeous Scottish accent
and James,
a guy from the Faroe Islands.
he was strumming softly on a guitar,
playing this and picking out that
as us girls just carried on either chatting or doing our
own thing
to this beautiful music playing in the background.
he started to play something
i recognized...

"Shallow" by Lady Gaga,
and asked if any of us knew the song.

and since he was over my bed on the top bunk,
the question was directed out to the other girls
visible from where he was sitting.
i'm not sure he even knew
i was there
on the bottom bunk beneath him.

i knew this song. by heart.

i started to sing quietly...
and he heard.
he leaned over the edge of the bed,
upside-down
and asked, "You know it?"
he smiled and said, "Sing with me,"
and started to sing Bradley Cooper's part.
when he got to Lady Gaga's part,
i wanted to belt out so loud
but i held it in.
oh, my diaphragm wanted to stretch to its max.
i wanted to sing.
i wanted to scream.
i wanted someone to hear these lyrics i had sung
time and time again
alone in my room
with tears falling down my face,
but i didn't...

"i'm off the deep end, watch as i dive in,
i'll never meet the ground
crash through the surface, where they can't hurt us
we're far from the shallow now..."
i sang, softly.
we sang together, sweetly.

i went back to writing in my journal
after we sang the song,
James continued strumming away
gently
a tune that held classical notes and soothed
our feminine souls.
the three of us applauded and begged, "encore!"

dive off the deep end,
you know how to swim...

day 23 - Mansilla de las Mulas to León

the wisdom of olga

18km/11mi to León today.

i walked with Olga from Germany,
the lady with the drippy poncho.

i was surprised to learn
(though i shouldn't have been, really
for nearly everyone here has such interesting stories)
she lived in the Spanish mountains with her baby girl
years ago,
strapped on her back, just as her pack is.

"every time I put it on, I think of those times with her,"
she said in her strong German accent
between the gap in her teeth.
"doing all of the day's work,
walking down to the river,
to town and back."

for two years, she lived like that.
"lived up there in the Spanish mountains,"
she said with pride.

as the enchanted witch i was picturing her to be,
she showed me which leaves
are good at preventing blisters...
"wrap them around your toes when you see hot spots
starting," she advised.
i took a few and put them in the front pockets of my
pack's waist strap.
she also picked a few yellow flowers
from the side of the road
that are good for digestion, and others that
are good if you have a sore throat.
"i'm going to give these to that girl over there,"

she had spotted someone from her yesterday's journey
who wasn't feeling so great...
"maybe these will make her feel better?"

a lady of 58 years from a tiny village near Hamburg,
Germany,
kept me going with stories that seemed like fairytales.

we walked through forests and valleys,
across ancient bridges and man-made roads of recent
stopping only for a larger-than-life,
freshly baked croissant
at a small bakery where
a sweet, apron-wearing lady stepped out and
greeted you with a warm smile.

we soon met up with sweet Choi from South Korea,
our roommate from a few albergues ago,
a chef-in-training living in Paris
with a smile like Daenerys,
the mother of dragons,
small but mighty,
for sure, she was.

over highways and walkways,
knowing we still had a couple miles to go until the
Plaza Mayor in León...

"anyone see cathedral spires yet?"

...we asked each other
as we walked closer and closer
to city center.

a sad farewell

this is where Mats and Monica's Camino ends.
León.
Monica's knees are hurting her too much to continue.
i am bummed.
beyond bummed,
i cried. Monica cried too.
but i understood.

we spent the afternoon and evening together,
sipping wine,
eating some of the best tapas in Spain...
bread and the most delicious olive oil on the planet,
roasted chicken on a bed of roasted red peppers
soaked in olive oil you better not think about wasting
(¡más pan, por favor!)
and tomatoes with avocado in the same
mouth-watering olive oil
only to be soaked up with more bread.

we walked through the streets of León, then
they took a rest in their hostel while
i met up with Suzanne to tour the cathedral.
we discussed grabbing dinner together,
mentioning Bekah and
wanting her there too.

a beautiful farewell.
or better yet, a

'til we see each other again.

note to self...

you're a good person.
you're a good mother.
you're a caring friend
and a sensual lover.
it's okay to just be,
to let yourself sink in,
breathe out the day's walk
and return within.
no matter what they say,
no matter what they think,
you'll never change any of it,
so why worry about it?
you're a good person,
even halfway around the world.
keep your heart open
and let the love unfurl.
keep your heart open,
even to the fear.
simply lean in
and allow it to be.
for it will
undeniably
reveal your truth, my dear.
reveal where you're aching and
need to heal.

the Spirit

"The most beautiful thing we can experience
is the mysterious."

- Albert Einstein

day 24 - León to Villar de Mazarife

the flight with werner

i set out from León
at 7:00 in the morning.
the sun rising over the cathedral
deepening my breath and awakening my soul.
following the familiar yellow arrows
that have led me this far,
i went this way and that, it was
a long walk out of the city
but not as long as the trek in,
thankfully.

as i approached the outer limits of León
there was a man, another pilgrim, walking ahead
of me...
he turned around and noticed i wasn't far behind.
he slowed his steps to let me catch up.
Werner was his name,
he was from Norway,
an older sturdy man
and an avid bird watcher
now retired and traveling the world to escape
Scandinavian winters.
his pace was unhurried
but steady
walking with no trekking poles
as confidently as a great heron
making its way through the marshes in the ebbs and
flows of the tides.
he told me many stories,
some of conversations he had had with other pilgrims
and how one should,
"walk at the pace of your soul."
i liked that.
those words resonated deep within me.
a kindred spirit.

i could get used to company like this.
and i love birds!
perfect walking companions.
birds have been my guardians along my Camino
thus far,
ever since starting in St. Jean Pied de Port.
i'm starting to believe they have stories too,
so i did my best to listen to them and
to all Werner was telling me about them.

we both stopped in Fresno del Camino
to rest and have another café con leche.
i asked to sit and have my coffee at his table,
something i rarely do...

i'd rather sit alone and people watch,
sit alone and feel safe in my own company,
sit alone and observe others from afar,
careful not to intrude on their space, time or energy,
or theirs on mine.
but his company was nice,
unassuming and gentle.
wise and welcoming.
i enjoyed the connection.
so i stayed.

a kindred presence is found

there is more here to be seen.
there is more here to believe.
so many stories and lessons i devour
at the touch of my soul, lasting forever.
sitting down next to a creek
for a bite to eat and observe the birds,
he teaches me things about life and love
reiterating beliefs my soul has always heard
deep down and from my spirit guides all around,
i know i'm in good company,
a kindred presence in him i've found.

journal entry: April 26, 2022

i walked with Werner today
an older pilgrim from Norway
and was entertained by intriguing conversations...
He told me story after story of fishing and
his friends asking,
"How was the fishing? Did you catch any fish?"
And he'd say,
"What fish? We were just drowning some worms."
(It's good to laugh)
He said
it's more about the experience and the company.
So true.
Isn't that what this is all about?
This Camino?
Life in general?
My untethered soul was being (re)threaded
by this man and his philosophies...

He pointed out bird after bird, explaining different things
about each one, which i really enjoyed.
The storks that build nests high on church steeples
and power lines,
the swallows who fly high when no rain's in the future,
the cuckoo who's difficult to see but easy to hear...

i'm in my albergue for the night -
it's a nice one with warm people.
i'm sitting here at the bar with a glass of wine, writing.
i love this. i want to continue this when i get home.
i've always been too shy to do this,
but i've learned that people aren't that interested in what
you're doing.
And it's okay.

Just do what makes your heart happy and
don't worry about what other people think.

kym's voice, loud and clear

i fell into the bathroom door
hurrying and not paying attention.
didn't see the tiny little step up and was anxious
to get in there,
(i thought i had started my period,
oh the joys of being female sometimes)
i tripped and fell right into the door frame and cut
my right forearm,
right into the middle of my bird tattoo.

(the tattoo i got for her, because of her, after she died...
i went to her tattoo artist
across town
lit a candle in her honor -
and my dad's honor, for he had just passed too -
and was permanently inked with seven silhouettes of
birds in flight,
flying through realms of transition,
from this life to the next)

the cut hurt so bad
i wanted to cry.
i wanted to call someone.
i wanted to vent, i wanted to scream...
it's times like these that i know Kym is near
doing what she said she'd do...
"wake the fuck up and be the lioness you are!"
is what i heard -
honesty and fearlessness.

thanks Kym, loud and clear.

day 25 - Villar de Mazarife to Hospital de Órbigo

i am listening

these heart rocks are
EVERYWHERE
i can't believe
how many
i've seen along the way.

they show up to speak to me
to let me know i'm loved,
i am love.
the Camino is love
and it is speaking to me.

speak freely, my friend.
i am listening.

journal entry: April 27, 2022

24 days walking, 13 to go...

*i had a somber night last night,
was feeling down, homesick, and guilty for being in such a
beautiful place, far from home.
But i slept well,
alone in a room meant for four.
No one to wake me,
no one to snore.*

*This morning
before leaving my albergue
the sweetest hospitalera greeted me with a smile at the bar,
made me a café con leche
and asked if she could take my photo as i was leaving.
Maybe she thought i looked like Pippi Longstocking
(like so many others since starting this hike)
or maybe she just liked me...
i'd like to believe the latter
for i really liked her too.
She walked me to the door,
we took a photo together
and hugged goodbye.
i expressed my gratitude for her kindness and my stay
and went on my way.*

What a beautiful start to my day.

*i ran into my Norweigan bird-watching friend, Werner,
today.
It was nice to walk and talk with him.
He showed me more birds and told me more stories.
Pointed out stork nests and motioned me to stop and listen
when he heard another cuckoo bird.
"You're lucky if you see them (the cuckoos), they hide.
But there are storks down on the ground there, hunting
worms, frogs, mice, for their*

babies up there in those nests," he said. "You see?"
i'd never seen such massive bird nests before.
Now i was obsessed with them,
finding them everywhere in the highest of peaks.

He was walking on to Astorga for the night
while i was staying in Hospital de Órbigo.
But before we parted ways,
we went for a coffee and a photo together,
exchanged numbers with him saying,
"If you're ever in Scandinavia, give me a call."
He promised to send me photos of the mushrooms
in his forest forages because
i've dreamt of searching for them in my forest dreams ...to go
to a Scandinavian country and look for forest mushrooms...
a nymph's dream come true.

All of these new friends along the Way
are like little homes to me. Comforting and warm,
welcoming
no matter how far i journey away
or how long it takes to return.

sweetness

beautiful weather and only 14km/8.5mi for me today,
since i wanted to stay
at a certain albergue -
Chardmo, a friend from high school
and my original inspo for the Camino,
said i must stay at the
Albergue Verde.
and i'm absolutely sure, this place is amazing.
warm and welcoming.
vegetarian/vegan.
they invited me in
immediately.
since i arrived so early, they offered me lunch
without asking for money yet either!
i was shown to my bunk
with the showers pointed out
and was encouraged to relax and
"make yourself at home."
a communal dinner and breakfast was explained,
all donativo.
the hospitalera was so sweet,
Cornelia,
from France but lives in Edinburgh, Scotland,
and speaks English, French, Spanish, Italian, German,
Mandarin,
and probably something else too.
and what an amazing cook she is.
for lunch, she made a
vegan tomato tart, a salad, delicious bread, and a sweet
potato puree.
she prepared rooibos tea and offered some (vegan)
chocolate cake that was
so delicious, i would've never guessed it was vegan.
she picked up everything off the table
even though i offered to help;
so did another pilgrim who had just arrived
and joined our impromptu lunch.
but no, Cornelia said, "you relax,"

so we did.
on the floor with pillows piling up all around us
in the colorfully decorated room for reflection.
i looked to the bookshelves at their collection...
this place overflowed with sweetness
and filled my heart.

my book!

i have some big news!!
my book's been accepted for publication!!
i am elated.
in shock.
so excited i can hardly breathe.
i'm texting family and friends
sharing in this amazingness.
i cannot hold it in,
i want to scream it
to the world and to
my albergue tonight
but i hold calm...
it's so peaceful here, i don't want to disturb anyone.
perhaps i'll share everything at dinnertime
for there's always the usual, "where are you from?"
"what brought you to the Camino?"
"what do you do back home?"

here's to good news and a good day.
(yes!
i am overflowing within)

gaztelugatxe?

dinner tonight at the Albergue Verde...
oven-roasted pumpkin slices with red onion, garlic,
olive oil, and salt,
the truest red beet hummus you've ever tasted,
delicious homemade bread, and a green salad with
a beautiful balsamic vinaigrette dressing.
no wine was served
(i am very sad to say)
this place is vegan -
and to my knowledge, no animals are harmed in the
making of wine?
but perhaps it's clarity they're after...
with the hot tea that was so nice.
warming the belly and soul,
as did the conversation.

i sat next to a guest of our hospitaleros,
a gentleman who would later lead us through a
meditation with
singing Tibetan bowls
in the yoga room (eek! i'm so excited).
with my elementary Spanish and his broken English,
we had a lovely conversation.
he asked where i was headed after reaching Santiago,
(for i had a week before i needed to be back in Paris
after making it to the great cathedral)
"will you walk on to Finisterre? the End of the World?"
i replied i wasn't sure...
i was beginning to doubt if my legs would carry me
to Finisterre.
"no? if not, where will you go before going home?"
yo no sé.
i asked where he was from
and he said, "Basque Country."
oh! Basque Country, one of my favorites so far!
he asked if i knew of Game of Thrones...
umm yeah, are you kidding me? i love that show!
"well, if you make it back to Basque Country,

go to Gaztelugatxe,
it's where they filmed Dragonstone."
really? you mean i'm this close?
i told him
and myself
that i will definitely keep this in mind...

Gaztelugatxe
stayed in the back of my mind as a possibility
for the days following
Santiago de Compostela to Paris...
but so did other cities, like Barritz and Porto.

**but still...
something about Gaztelugatxe
was calling me
and it wasn't just because
it was the setting for Dragonstone...**

exhausted

10:30pm and finally in bed.
after the singing bowl meditation and
having our credenciales stamped and signed,
paying what we thought was "reasonable"
for our radiant donativo stay at
Alberque Verde...

a quick bathroom visit and
it was time to sleep.

day 26 - Hospital de Órbigo to Astorga

journal entry: April 28, 2022

*Today's walk was beautiful to start
but took a turn for the worst
quickly.
Seems my bladder was angry with me -
Was it the tea last night after dinner?
Was it the constant pressure from my pack
strapped around my waist?
Or was my body in absolute protest over the miles and miles
i'd asked it
to carry me?*

*No
where
was there a place to stop...
not even a tree or a bush
for privacy
because people were everywhere,
pilgrims both ahead of me and behind me
without any break.
One after the other in their stream of walking
and
rightly so,
for i was on the
same path
but...*

*my bladder still screamed
and eventually
desperately
regrettably
undeniably and
uncontrollably
caved.*

My 20km/12.5mi hike into Astorga

ended
at Albergue de Peregrinos Siervas de María,
just inside town limits,
and
thank God
because (hands over face) my pants were so wet,
i was so embarrassed,
trying so hard to hide it with my jacket tied around my waist,
waiting in the corner
back against the wall
anxiously awaiting check-in
trying to hide until it was my turn
then politely hurrying the hospitalero by immediately
handing over
my passport, credenciales, and euros.

Completely awful.
So uncomfortable.
My intention was to make it a little further,
one more town or two up the road
but
my body said
NO.

i got to my room,
which i'm sharing with another American girl
who has a cold
(please don't pass it on to me).
So after our brief intros,
i kept my distance,
gathered my things
and showered,
washed my clothes and hung them to dry,
grabbed my journal
and headed straight for the Plaza Mayor.

i could get used to this

sitting here for a bit in
la Plaza Mayor de Astorga
writing
with a glass of wine.
feeling better
in dry clothes
and a humble spirit,
people-watching
with a plate of bread and meats
in front of me,
listening to three nearby ladies discussing plans
for the day
in Spanish...
thinking,
i wonder if they meet here every day
for a glass of wine
and a little (re)union?
wouldn't that be nice?
i'll get up and walk around in a minute,
i tell myself.
there's the Cathedral and Museo de Gaudi,
also el Museo de Chocolate
but first,
just breathe.
you're comfortable
and dry
and nourished.
enjoy this moment.

and i think of Hemingway,
wine and writing,
Pamplona,
no don't go back there,
don't miss him,
he's not here anymore.
he made his choice
and you must move on.
so i sit

alone in this plaza
picking out pilgrims by their attire,
socks in sandals,
freshly washed hair and face,
looking around at all the new sights to see
and smiling back.
i recognize you too.

i could get used to this.

day 27 - Astorga to Foncebadón

journal entry: April 29, 2022

*i had plans to stop in Rabanal del Camino today
and stay at the albergue where my high school friend
Chardmo and his uncle volunteered...
but there has been a group of girls and guys
so loud and obnoxious, walking
"with" me, not far ahead or behind me
for the past couple of days.
When i heard they were staying in Rabanal,
i decided to continue on.
i wanted to "lose" them, at least for tonight.
But now i'm wondering if it's them
or the Albergue Life i'm tiring of
because i'm equally annoyed by a couple of men sitting
next to me in this café of my albergue tonight
talking loudly
while i try to write and rest.
Maybe it's me growing weary of moving from
place to place.
Maybe it's me
just irritable today, perhaps.*

*i'm rooming with 5 other people,
two of which are personable and nice.
a young couple from South Korea,
Jessie and Chun.
They're on their honeymoon and walking the Camino.
Can you imagine?
Sleeping in separate twin beds almost every night in a room
full of pilgrims.
i'm not sure i would've done the same.
i'm impressed and in admiration.*

*The climb to Foncebadón today was 5km of steep struggle,
up rocks and slats of stone.
Achingly breathtaking*

in the most physical way
but beautiful,
WOW so beautiful to the eye.
And to the spirit.
Just what i needed to wear my sharp edges down today.

day 28 - Foncebadón to Molinaseca

from covid

the day my father died
from covid,
two days before Christmas last year
from covid,
i was standing in line at a testing facility
to be tested
for covid,
for the third time
so hospice would let me back in
to see him
one last time
but he was dying
already

from covid.

why did it matter?
i seethingly wondered.
what did it matter?
i could care less about anyone else
at this moment.
my dad,
my father,
was dying
in a facility
all by himself
wrapped in plastic,
doors and windows tightly shut,
no life allowed,
is this how it has to be?

the memory of him
just a couple weeks prior
standing inside the house,
his back turned to the door

watching tv,
sick
from covid.
my mother
quarantined
in the same house,
with covid.
i knocked on the door
trying to get his attention
to say hi,
i love you,
be strong,
you'll be okay,
but he didn't hear me.
i thought about ringing the doorbell
but he was deathly unsteady on his feet
and
i didn't want to startle him.
why didn't i startle him?
why didn't i ring that doorbell?

that was the last time i saw him
conscious.
that was the last time i saw him
unconsumed
from covid.

days later
i saw his pain
through regulation-required goggles,
drapes and gowns and N-95 masks
and gloves,
plastic touching plastic,
humans looking like aliens in
rooms that were guarded and
barricaded,
as if all feeling was illegal,
any skin-to-skin contact would clip your wings and
and shatter you to pieces.
but i was already in pieces
and my feelings and his

were synchronized with tears.
"don't wipe them away,"
i was warned,
"when you're in there,
don't touch your face
and don't touch his."

he cried out ever so softly,
"help, sabrie"
and time stopped.

this isn't life -
how can anything survive this?

in the hospital,
no nurses came.
in the hospital,
no doctors came.
everyone was scared of him
and what he could transmit.
they didn't care, it seemed,
this is my father!
my screams faded in the silence.
how can you be so cruel?!
he'll never survive this.
how can anyone survive this?

he died.
from covid.
while i stood in line
testing for covid.
i got the call from my brother
and the world blurred out.

the pain, the confusion,
the anger, the guilt.

**i'm sorry you died this way, Dad. i'm sorry
you died alone in that room,
from covid.**

el cruz de ferro

all alone. at this magnificent place.
where pilgrims have been
placing stones for centuries, as
a symbol of letting go,
of leaving something behind that has burdened them
for far too long.
and not only stones,
but notes and shoes and pictures of loved ones,
anything that has been with them all along the Way
from here to there.
some people bring stones from home,
others pick up stones along the path.
i brought mine from home,
for i knew about this place and knew
this stop would be significant,
i knew immediately
what i wanted to leave,
knew immediately
why and how
i wanted to leave them.

four stones...
that sat on my desk at home,
the home i let go of in the divorce,
the stones i looked at every day
when i wrote and worked
in my journal and on my book
from the day covid shut the world down,
sending my (now ex) husband home out of work
for 2 years,
through my parents in the hospital with covid,
my dad dying,
through Kym's imminent and devastating death
from cancer,
to the final days of my marriage.
a marriage i knew was in trouble
but would've done anything to save.

it was out of my hands.
it was all out of my hands.
just like these stones.
they've been through it all with me
right there on my desk.
they gave me strength
they gave me light
they reflected the sun
and shared in the moon.
these gorgeous crystals
told me everything would be okay.
clear quartz
rose quartz
aventurine
and citrine...
i placed them
surrounded by one of my white-beaded bracelets
on the high mountain of "gifts"
now out of my hands.

Dad's death.
Kym's death.
my divorce.
and the writing of my novel, page by page.
i let them all go
as i let these stones go
as tears flooded my eyes and let themselves go
all over my red cheeks and soaked face
from sadness to acceptance,
from honoring their memories to finding
perseverance.
they are now with the Spirit of the Camino
always and forever.
they are out of my hands
and i am okay with it.
it is a comforting thought,
them being held here in the energy of el Cruz de Ferro.
they've served their purpose with me...
perhaps they'll find their way to someone else
and serve them too.

i'm okay

last night
i had a dream that Jude and i
were okay.
not back together
but okay.
we hugged,
understanding each other,
having shared a kinship of sorts.

i wasn't sad
when the dream ended,
i was okay with its ending
as i'm okay with the divorce.
as much as it still hurts to say.
i forgive him and i forgive myself,
it wasn't working
and i'm okay with it.
i hope he's okay too,
if it's okay to say.

just a question...

if things had been different,
would we be different now?

standing tall

in between
stumbling from
Cruz de Ferro
to finding a place to rest
in Molinaseca for the night,
i met Erik, from Denmark.
he spotted me sitting and resting on a ledge
taking a sip of water
in the rising temperatures and sunshine
of today's walk through forests and small villages.
he asked if i was okay,
if i needed anything.
i told him i was fine, just resting.
and he sat with me for a bit.
told me of his day.
why he was here,
like the rest of us,
trying to figure it all out...
said he didn't feel appreciated at home
by his kids or his wife.
said his wife was all too happy to see him leave
for this Camino.
laughing a bit to shake off the hurt
but his pain showed through
and i sympathized.

i know every relationship
has its hard times. but
the question is,
...how do you get back?
i wanna know.
for my future relationship.
for my future Love.
for the inevitable seas that lie ahead of trials and trust.
i want to love and be loved.
i wanna know.

we talked about my book

and that i'd heard from a publisher,
a hybrid publisher...
Erik advised, "be careful,
read over that contract carefully.
have a lawyer look at it before you sign."
but with that advice came encouragement too,
"I'm so happy for you though! that's a **h u g e**
accomplishment.
you should be proud!"

i stood a little taller as i walked.
head held high.

the only pilgrim

hiking down from el Cruz de Ferro...

hold on,
let me put that another way...

i cried,
stumbled,
crawled in the most upright position
one could ever crawl,
for fear of falling
and breaking something,
not being able to move or be found for hours.
i felt every rock
every stone
every crack in the hard earth
beneath each foot.
and pavement wasn't any better
once i reached some.
my body was as tired as my soul.
carrying the hurt, the loss, the wounds to patch up
the holes in my heart,
i needed a place to rest.

in a sea of places
amongst this riverbed village called Molinaseca,
i was the only pilgrim
in an albergue i found
with 24 beds,
a hospitalero and his dog.

journal entry: April 30, 2022

The climb to the Iron Cross,
el Cruz de Ferro,
where i left my stones and
everything else i needed to leave
was hard.
Followed by a

long

long

descent

down rocks

and slats

and tears

and exhaustion,

all of the day

down

down

until i reached Molinaseca.

i thought i could go further
but again
my body,
mind and spirit
disagreed.
i found a charming albergue where
i believe
i'm the only one staying overnight.

This man, this hospitalero, is so kind,
him and his dog, Rosie.
He made me dinner, pasta salad with veggies and tuna,
ribs (which i didn't have the heart to say "i don't really care
for those") with fries,
un postre, a delicious chocolate cake, and a
whole bottle of vino tinto.
Served with a smile,
as i believe he's as happy to have company
as i am.

A quiet night and a good dinner
with a gracious host,
good for the soul after being alone with my tears
all day.
Not only was it a hard day physically
but emotionally, as well.
Letting go at el Cruz de Ferro then
hearing from my kids that things are hard at home...
i feel helpless.
There's nothing i can do from over here.
All i can do is hope that they're strong enough
from what they've (hopefully) learned from me
to make it through.

i believe they are...
they're half of me.

strangers

i wonder
if we've lost the ability to trust
in strangers in America?

in an albergue,
me, the only pilgrim, with
the only other person, the hospitalero (and his dog).
he cooked me a pilgrim's meal,
made a fire in the wood stove as the sun set
and brought an extra blanket in "just in case."
he slept in the room across the hall,
only a set of stairs on either side
separating us,
a floor to ceiling tapestry of an elephant
in all her majesty
lit by the moon seeping through the windows
and around the corners,
and even though i woke a few times to his snoring
(it was pretty loud, to be honest)
i never woke for fear.
i never felt unsafe.
not once.
there were cracks and creaks and noises
throughout the house
that would unnerve most people,
(that would unnerve me in most settings)
but i knew i was safe.

but why did i feel safe?

thousands of miles from home
in a near-empty place
sleeping overnight
by myself?
every voice from my learned childhood
screamed
"you shouldn't feel safe here,"
but i did.

and it makes me wonder...

why don't we trust before not trusting?
why do we assume the worst in people before allowing
possibility to filter in?

the pink house

as quiet as a mouse
you come and go,
no trace of where you've been
or to where you'll go,
just the memory of a moment
for the lifetime of your soul,
as quiet as a mouse
you depart and unfold.

day 29 - Molinaseca to Cacabelos

journal entry: May 1, 2022

*9 days to Santiago and it's like the towns
get livelier and livelier.
Sitting (again) with a glass of wine
and writing,
(seems to be my m.o. for afternoons here in Spain)
at an outdoor table of the bar where my albergue is
for the night.
(These bars with albergues upstairs are so adorable.)*

*My walk today was so much
better
than yesterday.
No knee-killing, soul-crushing descents today.
A few tough stretches
but nothing like yesterday.*

*i reached Cacabelos for the day/night
and WOW! People are EVERYWHERE.
Today is Market Day,
but this is SO much bigger than Market Day in
Carrión de Los Condes.
Street after street, vendor after vendor,
corner after corner
all crammed with people, so many people
coming in by cars
and cars everywhere.
Shops and restaurants full to the brim,
so full with no room to explore
that i decided to turn around and return to
my home for the night
and write.*

*i can't believe it's May 1st already.
Twenty days and i'll be back home.
i miss my kids and can't wait to see them.*

i miss Bella and the kitties too,
i wonder how things will be with Paul when i return...
We still text and are friends, i guess,
in a way, though it feels weird and unnatural.
i won't worry about it,
though, it is puzzling.
i know i'll be sad to leave Europe.
i love life here.
The towns, the people, the history, the languages,
finding a plaza to sit and have a glass of wine and
contemplate the day.
This is the life, isn't it?
i do miss home though
and having a home.

This morning after waking and packing up,
my host made me a larger than usual cup of coffee,
an enormous piece of toast
from a gloriously-made fresh loaf of bread
and placed a candy bar next to my bag...
then brought in a second,
"You the only peregrina, no?"
(meaning he had extra and wanted to share)
i smiled and replied, "Tú eres muy amable."

When it was time for me to go, he locked up
and leashed Rosie to walk with me for a kilometer or so.
He told me his tales of walking the Camino,
14 times, with Rosie too!
and showed me photos of him and her in front of the
cathedral.
Inspiring and sweet.

He didn't know me from another pilgrim,
and i didn't know him from any other person.
But somehow there was trust
and it took me back to that question in my head...
Could this happen in the States?
i mean, the amount of care and concern,
trust, and safely returns?

day 30 - Cacabelos to Ambasmestas

galicia, evermore

green hillsides
climbing mountains
winding rivers that sing to you along the way,
flocks of sheep grazing
as if right out of a Mary's Little Lamb nursery tale,
old buildings ready with their own stories to tell
with trees so old and bent, their stories
would be a language too ancient to decode.
another lifetime would i need
to read all their words and history...
but a challenge i am ready and willing to
accept, for this is the journey i signed up for,
this is the journey my soul has been craving,
evermore.

journal entry: May 2, 2022

24km/15mi from Cacabelos today.
And an absolutely gorgeous day at that.
Vineyard after vineyard,
nothing to hear but birds singing their morning songs and
the sound of my own footsteps
along a path that imitated the rolling hills.

About 8km/5mi in this morning,
i reached Villafranca and
stopped at a small café for a coffee and bit of breakfast.
When i walked into the bar,
there were men sitting at a table who looked at me in
somewhat of amazement
and made me laugh inside.
i placed my order and went to the aseos.
When i came out,
one man held up a photo of Pippi Longstocking
and pointed to me.
i laughed,
he laughed
then looked at me again,
asking of my relation to her.
"No," i said, "no relation," and laughed again too.
These braids are simply a super easy way to keep my hair
out of my face.
(In all the unexpected weather here on the Camino,
my hair was the last thing i wanted to worry about.)
Flattered, i smiled and said,
"Thank you."
Pippi Longstocking is a free spirit
i feel honored to be compared to.

i sat down outside
with my coffee and tortilla
next to a medieval castle that i was dying to explore
but didn't have time to.
So i sat

enjoying mi desayuno,
thinking about my book and seeing it on shelves!
and seven swallows flew overhead.
SEVEN.
Just like my tattoo.
Warm chills brushed my forearms and raced
through and through.

i hear you, Kym. Loud and clear.
Thanks for the encouragement.
Forever and always, my girl.

A father/daughter pilgrim team stopped to say
good morning and Buen Camino!
and to ask how i was doing.
i chatted with them for a bit
then they were on their way.
Americans too.
i picked up on the accent and mannerisms.

After Villafranca, the Way turned
from dirt paths through vineyards
to sidewalks and concrete.
Tough on the legs and
tougher on the feet.

day 31 - Ambasmestas to Liñares

o cebreiro

eating breakfast
in my quiet Ambasmestas hotel, and
who comes walking through the door looking for un
café y un baño but
Suzanne!
so of course we walk together today,
up the long, steep stretch to O Cebreiro.

the climb to O Cebreiro
makes even the seasoned hiker's thighs burn.
step after step
up 620 meters
on a dirt track
that's used by farmers and herd animals alike,
noticing the hoof prints accompanying your steps,
you duck under overhanging brush,
careful not to snag your leg on nettles sticking out,
placing one foot in front of the other,
again and again.
stopping to catch your breath
you turn around and survey your surroundings.
people in front and people in back...
you step aside,
gathering your breath
and your next bit of strength for yet
another part of the climb.

soon you realize
you're climbing with the world
around you,
you feel the energy from the ground
lifting you higher and higher.
energy so big and supportive,
loving and sometimes humorous,
you laugh about the difficulty and chat about

what you'll do at the top
when you're finally able to sit for a while.

you could not do this climb alone.
i could not do this climb alone.
i suppose you or i could but...
you need those beautiful souls around you
to keep you going.
you need that energy around you
to keep you going.
the spirit of those past and
the spirit of those ahead.

when we reached the top,
there were many others
catching their breath
and sitting.
resting. before
walking into O Cebreiro
which feels like
walking into one of the most magical villages yet
on the Camino.
stone streets
and buildings to match
with thatched roofs and a feeling of
walking back in time,
cafés and bars set tightly within each other
and short doorways even i had to duck to enter.

and, of course,
the church at the top -
a soul's haven.

Suzanne and i walked into the church and,
when i say it held the sweetest spirit ever,
i'm not lying.
it wasn't overdone with gold or silver,
it wasn't pompous or pretentious,
it was modest
and humble
with soft music playing and monks singing

in the background,
offering peacefulness,
like a mother's arm to a tired child.

an older couple, standing as volunteers,
stamped our credenciales and asked,
"where are you from?"
the gentleman explained the history of the naming of
Florida when he heard my answer.
sadly, i can't remember what he said,
but they offered me a private pilgrim blessing
and that...
i do remember.

the lady showed me where to rest my pack
and walked me to the altar,
giving me a piece of paper with
the Prayer of La Faba
printed in English.

she asked me to read it,
saying,
"i'm so sorry for my poor English."
(oh my heart)
i'm so sorry for my poor Spanish!

after reading the prayer out loud,
she gave me a tiny rock
with a yellow arrow painted on it.
"whenever you look at it or hold it,"
she said in slow but good English,
"you will remember this Pilgrim Blessing."
and it's true.
i do.

i have it with me today.

the prayer of la faba

Although I may have traveled all the roads,
crossed mountains and valleys from East to West,
if I have not discovered the freedom to be myself,
I have arrived nowhere.

Although I may have shared all of my possessions
with people of other languages and cultures;
made friends with Pilgrims of a thousand paths,
or shared albergues with saints and princes,
if I am not capable of forgiving my neighbour tomorrow,
I have arrived nowhere.

Although I may have carried my pack from beginning to end
and waited for every Pilgrim in need of encouragement,
or given my bed to one who arrived later than I,
given my bottle of water in exchange for nothing;
if upon returning to my home and work,
I am not able to create brother(sister)hood
or to make happiness, peace and unity,
I have arrived nowhere.

Although I may have had food and water each day,
and enjoyed a roof and shower every night;
or may have had my injuries well attended,
if I have not discovered in all the love of God,
I have arrived nowhere.

Although I may have seen all the monuments
and contemplated the best sunsets;
although I may have learned a greeting in every language;
or tried the clean water from every fountain;
if I have not discovered who is the author
of so much free beauty and so much peace,
I have arrived nowhere.

If from today I do not continue walking on your path,
searching for and living according to what I have learned;
if from today I do not see in every person, friend or foe

a companion on the Camino;
(if from today I cannot recognize God,
the God of Jesus of Nazareth
as the one God of my life,)
I have arrived nowhere.

—

on the piece of paper i read out loud in the church,
the lines in parenthesis above were not there.
my guess was to include as many people,
as many religious beliefs as possible
into this one prayer.
and honestly,
it fits.

we all walk this Way for different reasons,
whether religious/spiritual or other.
and in all my days on this trail so far,
i've come to the conclusion
that every single person has a reason
for being here.
it's not just a vacation
or a cheap way to explore Spain.
there is something deeper here bringing people from
all over the world together
here
on the Camino.
and whether you believe in God or not,
whether you're Christian or not,
at one point
along your Way
you will meditate and reach
some higher state of mind
and just
be.

what's it all for?

after stopping for lunch
with James (the guitar guy), Suzanne, and a couple of
other Camino friends
we continued on towards Liñares
where Suzanne and i were stopping for the day -
James told us
he was continuing on to a village or two further
up the way.

it didn't take long for our conversation
as we walked
to steer more towards the philosophical
as we stopped
to take in the mountainous views,
James, Suzanne, and i ...

he asked a question
i hadn't been asked yet here on the Camino,
"so what do you think the meaning of life is?"
he laughed a bit,
"isn't that what we're here to figure out?
haven't you been asked that question yet?"
no, I haven't.
and yeah, it is, i laughed
and gave it some thought.
walked, thinking for a minute,
"i guess it's this", opening my arms to everything
around us, "community,
spending time with others
and allowing people into your world,
trusting, loving..." i trailed off.
he smiled and agreed, as did Suzanne.
they each gave their own variation of the same.
it's so true,
life is more than stuff and money.
"life is about experiencing,"
we all agreed.

here on the Camino
you're flooded with experiences,
soft and hard
easy and tiresome
happy and sad,
every bit of what life is.
some things must die in order for others to begin again,
the cycle,
the thread,
the weaving in and out,
the ebbs and flows,
yet everything you need is right at your fingertips.
you soon realize how little you actually need,
material-wise,
day to day
to get by.
it's the connections
the community around you
the support and the love
that keep you going,
that matters most.

i asked James the age-old question,
"so what brought you here?"
after telling us it's his second Camino in 2 years,
"i needed to get away for while and walk..."
he explained how his mother was ill,
how his business with a friend was going under,
then the kicker, perhaps...
the third reason why he was here...
"there's a girl back home who's pregnant
with my child."
and the struggle inside him was -
"do I leave my job and move back home, risk not
making enough money?"
or
"remain a father but from a distance
and risk not knowing my child as i want?"

everyone
has a storm to weather,

(but we can stay afloat
if we paddle together.)

that's what this is all about,
what i've come to know
so far.

patience

when Suzanne and i got settled into our albergue,
we went down to the local store and bought things
to make dinner.
pasta with tomato sauce and mushrooms,
bread and olive oil
and wine, of course,
oh! but of course.

—

i've received a lot of advice
regarding my book and its publication.
so to sift through the pieces,
i reached out to a friend of a friend,
a published author who has a lot of experience
and she offered a little tidbit…
"be patient. keep trying. it'll be worth it in the end."

so that's what i'm doing…
being patient.
onwards and upwards,
always and forever.
ultreia et suseia.

day 32 - Liñares to Samos

journal entry: May 4, 2022

6 days to Santiago...

Today started out in the clouds,
fog so thick you couldn't see a meter in front of you,
all you could hear were little dew droplets
falling
against the leaves on the trees,
as the sun began to rise
the clouds began to disappear, as if
happy to be here but sleepy and
wanting to skip the opening act.
It was a long day's hike for me today,
28km/17mi.
Suzanne and i parted ways
since she had to get to Santiago two days before me
to catch her flight back home in time.
She was going a different way at this point and
i wanted to walk through Samos,
a slightly longer
but more beautiful way along the river and forests,
(all the books seemed to say).
But after nearly the entire 28km,
the sound of the river was the only thing carrying me.
i forgot where i was,
paid little attention to where I was going,
my energy was so low
and i desperately needed to rest.
i was slow and sluggish and full of tears
about to fall from exhaustion
but received encouraging words from fellow pilgrims,
"only a little further to go,"
and it helped, but i was done.
mentally, physically, spiritually.
i was tired and my legs were aching
down to the bone.

i wanted to cry
and so i did.

then i saw smoke billowing from chimneys ahead
and realized i had arrived in Samos.
my spirit lifted as relief came over me.
i was happy.

When i walked into the monastery,
Albergue de Peregrinos Monasterio de Samos,
i was greeted with, "ah! you made it!"
from the encouraging pilgrim a few hamlets back
and i smiled.
Enchanting but
donativo only,
so bare minimum
and so COLD!
OH so cold. No heat.
But the smiles made up for it.
Shelter, hot water, a toilet, and
a place to lay my head.
Everything i needed
and nothing to fret.

i was so hungry when i arrived at 3:30pm
that after my shower, i went out to find food...
of course, i found a friendly bar with wine and a
delicious bocadillo con jamón y queso.
i sat in the shade with my journal, a pen, and my sandwich.
"Ah, the writer!",
said a passing pilgrim
who recognized me and my journal.

if i may say so...
that's so nice to hear.

day 33 - Samos to Barbadelo

breathing again

Galicia is
a magical place.
a place that falls right out of your childhood dreams
right into the pack on your back
with hopes of a new love and a gentle kiss
as you dance into the very real mist...

you remember -
how beautiful you are
how magnificent this earth is
how resilient you've become
how much love we all need
and how much love surrounds us all at any given time.

with stone bridges and ancient forests,
eucalyptus trees soaring through the sky
filling every inch of your sensory body with a scent
that reminds you of home
and of comfort so near.

as your mind begins to awaken
through the foggy mornings of walking
past farmhouses and fires brewing,
the day lightens
and the fog lifts,
your mind opens and your heart begins
to beat again.

**as you begin to breathe the world around you,
the world breathes out, (re)filling you too.**

sarria

100km until Santiago.
this is the place many people start walking
in order to get their Compostela.
but my credenciales was full, and
i needed to stop in the Pilgrim Office just as i was
getting into town
for another.
she was kind and welcoming, and smiled so brightly
when she saw i had a full book already.
stamped to start me again from here,
i set out to find lunch and give my brother a call to
wish him "happy birthday!"
"salud! love you!"
so very close
though thousands of miles away.

journal entry: May 5, 2022

In a very small town tonight
so small, there's not even a single store,
no restaurant,
only two albergues
and a church that was built in c. 865...
(hard to wrap my mind around that one!)
So i had to walk to the town just before this one for
dinner and wine.
It's ok, it's only a 5 minute walk,
and a gorgeous one at that...
staring into green valleys across even greener pastures
illuminated by a coming sunset.
i see roads way off in the hilly distant with cars rushing by
and think... i'm happy to be here
and not in a hurry somewhere.
i like this pace.
i like walking to my dinner.
i like this simplicity and knowing i have just what i need.

Today was only about 19-20km/12mi,
my legs and feet needed a shorter day today.
Perhaps tomorrow i'll go a bit longer.

Reaching Sarria came with a mix of emotions.
Happy to finally make it this far
but sad to have reached the final stretch.
i should be in Santiago in less than a week,
so i want to take my time and sip all there is left to enjoy...
but i also want to celebrate in the excitement of reaching
Santiago with newly-made friends -
which means keeping up the pace.

And speaking of friends...

i was now at dinner with myself,
enjoying a glass of wine and my first course of
stuffed peppers with rice in an amazing tomato sauce AND

goat cheese toasts topped with caramelized onions and
balsamic dressing...
Delicious.
and who do i see??
Jacey!!!

i was hoping i'd run into her again and
here she was!

We had the BEST time tonight catching up,
laughing
crying
venting
reminiscing...
We told stories and laughed some more.
Paper towels! I found some in a bathroom recently,
what luxury! (laughing.)
i shared my wine and food with her
and she decided to order a little something and join me
for dinner.
We went inside
to get away from the chilling evening temperatures,
drank more wine
and laughed the night away.

i received a text from Choi while at dinner, as well.
She's already in Portomarín,
a town i'll pass through tomorrow.
Fingers crossed our paths cross again!

Beautiful souls, beautiful friends.

day 34 - Barbadelo to Castromayor

hamlets and abodes

these tiny, little hamlets
throughout Galicia
are the heart of the area.
only a few cobble houses,
a dairy farm and its inhabitants,
sometimes a small chapel
and always a farmer
working his hands into the ground.

pilgrims come and go,
but not much else changes
in these earthy abodes.

journal entry: May 6, 2022

4 days to Santiago!

i could've stayed back in Portomarín,
which was a cool town,
but i'm growing weary of large crowds in albergues.
So i walk,
i just walk,
i walk ahead
until i find the first albergue with a restaurant inside
because i can't bear to walk anymore.

The towns between the "larger" ones are very small now.
Almost nothing to them,
a farm, a handful of old houses,
maybe a store or tiny café that's open for just a short while,
of course a church,
and
if you're lucky...
an albergue.

This village tonight,
Castromayor,
is only 9km from Portomarín
and the hospitalera is so sweet but speaks even less English
than i speak Spanish.
It's okay though, we'll get by.
Jacey should be joining me too,
which i'm very much looking forward to.

The last two hours of today's hike were harsh.
Continuous walking down a sidewalk
along a busy highway,
a sprinkle of forests in between a few hills,
up and down
and around several bends
and for the most part, no shade.
A rare tree offered some

but it was crowded with sweaty hikers
panting and sipping water
complaining of the heat, and i get it -
the sun was hitting extra hot today.

i should probably start looking ahead
into the next few days and
figure out where i'll be and make reservations.
But i rather like throwing the dice and letting the Camino
choose where i land for the day.
They say it gets busier, the last 100km, and that
it's hard to find places to stay...
but i'm gonna take my chances.

i do know i should book my stay in Santiago
and start thinking about how i'm getting back
to Paris...
seems like a lot of work that i don't want to do right now,
nor do i want this to end,
but i must
and it must,
like everything in life...

We have beginnings
only and when
we have endings.

no, it wasn't a dream

i showered
to wash the day's sweaty heat off.
i washed my clothes
and hung them out
to dry beneath the trees
noticing the green pastures
around me,
the cows grazing peacefully as the wind
soaked up the dying sunlight
and cooled the sunny patches.
could it get any more serene than this?
clothes on a line
drying in the sun,
a gracious host inside
preparing me a pilgrim's dinner
with wine
and a quiet dining room to write
and reflect...

then i see Nevo walk in.
there goes the quiet.

Nevo, the young, talkative Israeli i met back in
Terradillos de Los Templarios.
he sat down at my table and asked,
"how are you?"
he said he had already made it to Santiago...
(what?!)
"why are you here?" i asked.
"i'm here," explaining in his thickly-accented English,
"to get money from Erik."
i saw Erik walk in.
well if this journey doesn't get more and more
interesting
every day.
apparently Erik is friends with Nevo's mom,
who was walking the Camino, as well, but was a few
towns back.

"yeah i need some money so my mom gave it to Erik,"
he explained.
i was beginning to see the invisible web weaving
around me.

this community of pilgrims
so big
but so small and intimate.
we had grown to know each other
by one way or another,
like the threads of a spider's web,
numerous and in different orientations,
all meeting in the center,
traveling in the same general direction.
someone had met another and that another was friends
with this person...
this person knew that person and that person was
connected
to someone else.
it's amazing.
no matter the degrees of separation,
we're all connected on this path
along the Way.

Jacey came in to sit with me while i ate,
providing a buffer between me and Nevo
(which i was ever so grateful for).
Nevo said he was taking a taxi back to Santiago tonight
(again, thank God)
but before he left, he filled us in on quite the eventful
night he had had...

one night,
partying with other hikers
he said, he had had a lot to drink
and was high too
and thought he could walk through the night
along the Camino
in complete darkness,
except for his headlamp.
(Jacey and i looked at each other, "not a smart

idea, dude." the rocky hazards... the sides of the
road/mountain you could fall off of... the chance you'd
miss a turn or a fork in the path and get lost...
at night? dude...)
he said he was doing fine
until he came upon a group of dogs...
they looked friendly at first,
but then they started chasing him.
growling, snarling, snapping at him as they got closer
and closer.
he said he just knew they were going to catch up and
attack him.
but something came over him,
he paused...
then continued,
"I stopped and looked at them...
all of a sudden, they weren't growling anymore.
they walked up to me and licked my hands. they were
my friends.
a man came running out of the field nearby,
screaming at me, chasing after me,
and my new friends, these dogs,
chased after him. they protected me!"

when he left,
Jacey and i paused,
looked at each other,
"some wine?"

day 35 - Castromayor to San Xulian

3 days to santiago

feeling the sweet pains of sad excitement
in these last few days...

i feel my body begging for a long rest as
my feet and knees take pound after pound of more
pavement and stones,
hour after hour.

but even through the exhaustion,
my spirit wants to climb
higher and higher
as my soul summits peaks
it's never reached before.

only 3 days to Santiago.

journal entry: May 7, 2022

Such a strange feeling -
my time on the Camino is quickly coming to an end.
My body is tired.
My legs and feet
my knees
are aching.
i cannot go long distances anymore.
i feel myself looking forward to a rest,
a deep rest,
but on the other hand,
i'm very sad it's coming to an end.
This rhythm of walking,
packing, walking, eating, walking again,
finding a place to stay,
and sleeping...
only to get up and do it all over again
the next day
is what i needed.
Is what i feel i'm still needing.
This catharsis.
i've learned a lot from this time
and i hope it stays with me
in the days and months to come and
for a very, very long time.
And when i feel it starting to fade,
maybe it'll be time to return
again.
Yes, just maybe...

i'm not going to rush to Santiago,
though i do feel its pull,
a push
to Santiago,
from those around me and to where we're going.
i've mapped it out, 3 more days to get there
comfortably.
Taking my time

slowly.

But where should i stay?
All of my friends have their places lined up,
some are even there at the Cathedral already.
Do i splurge and stay in the Parador or
do i find something more economical,
pilgrim-budget friendly?

Thinking, thinking
researching,
researching...

Ok... airbnb is booked in Santiago!
My mind wouldn't rationalize paying that much
for the Parador,
even though it's breathtaking and
a beautiful experience, i'm sure.
i'll stay somewhere a little more comfortable in my wallet,
very near the Cathedral and the four plazas surrounding it.
And it's right above a chocolate bar, HELLO!
is there anywhere better? i don't think so.
it was the first to pop up in my search
and i went with it.

The Camino provides.
Indeed it does.

so far

in this adorable village for the night...
with *The Right Words* book in hand
(a gift from Jane and Quino, my fellow elephant lover
and artist friend back in Madrid),
a carafe of red wine and
dinner being prepared by another lovely couple
of hospitaleros
on the way out...
i am content.
the weather is beautiful,
a constant breeze
blowing dandelion blooms up and around the trees,
circling the stone-built homes,
floating between the tables and chairs
journeying down the street
with a handful of pilgrims as they pass by,
a tractor trailing its happy dog in the back
on their way home before the night's sky.
sunny and warm enough for a short-sleeve shirt,
a black and white cat sits by my side below my chair,
purring in the wind.
a full plate of pasta with pesto is brought out
and i write...
thinking of Kym,
how she would've loved this.

i'm glad i lost my ring in Azofra.
Kym is now a part of the Camino,
just as i am.

our Camino.

she's walked with me this whole way,
so far...

this is your Camino too, i whisper to the wind.
yes, this i know so far, my friend.

day 36 - San Xulian to Arzúa

journal entry: May 8, 2022

i walked a little further than planned today,
thanks to one of Jacey's 600mg ibuprofens.
i reached the town i was planning on staying in tonight,
Arzúa.

When we sat and had lunch earlier,
two salads that looked amazing to these two pilgrims who
were so used to breads, meats, and cheeses...
Jacey noticed a live caterpillar in hers.
When i took it in to the restaurant and explained,
"un gusano en la ensalada,"
the lady got so distressed.
It seemed she didn't want to believe me,
but she wouldn't take my money either.
i tried to communicate in Spanish as best i could,
but it hurt me knowing i had hurt her feelings
or offended her or her business somehow.

i laughed nervously to Jacey about it
when i returned to the table -

People have bad days
all over the world,
and i reminded myself of that.

Maybe this lady was having a bad day...
i'm sure we pilgrims can be quite annoying at times.
So i didn't press the issue
and we simply moved on.
We ate some snacks we had in our packs,
a few cookies and a handful of crackers,
a piece of chocolate and a sip of our waters.
Jacey gave me one of her ibuprofens
because my legs were aching quite a bit, and we
kept on

walking.

We arrived in Arzúa
and i said i'd look for an albergue here.
Jacey gave me a hug,
***¡Buen Camino! I'll see you in Santiago!** she said*
and carried on to do the 30km/18.6mi today she said she
needed to do.
25km/15.5mi was good enough for me.

i found an albergue
but it was full.
The girl at check-in said she had another,
same price (12 euros), clean, if i wanted it.
YES please.

She walked me there personally
and gave me my own room in a very quiet albergue
just up the road.
Heaven.
This girl was heaven-sent,
she must've seen the tired look on my face
or the inner breaking-downs of my body inside
for she didn't have to be so gracious.
No other smelly people tonight,
no snorers,
no one to wake me by coming in late,
i thanked her over and over again
and looked forward to my sleeping well
tonight...

mother's day (in america)

it was good to see my kids' smiling faces
over facetime.
they "sent" me
smiles, lots of love, encouraging words
and a heart-shaped strawberry
ready to be dipped in chocolate <3

i love being their mother.

no more blurry lines

i talked with Paul after dinner...
(the conversation we needed to have.)
it's been confusing to me
staying in contact and
not being in a relationship
after we had been so close,
all the questions i still had
in my mind,
it's like trying to rewind a tape with your fingers,
only to get them stuck
and all tangled up.
i needed to know
exactly
where things were.
spell it out.
draw the line.
rip the bandage off, if needed.
for i could not complete my Camino on lies,
on false hope,
on a pretense that everything was fine,
because it didn't feel fine.
none of this felt fine.
he told me
he didn't believe we were right for each other,
that eventually he wanted to see other people.
those words hurt,
especially the latter,
for they were new to me.
our talks thus far had ended with
"we'll see when you get home" or
"i see a future for us
but I just don't know what kind yet."
it was open-ended
and confusing.
it wasn't what i was wanting,
it wasn't what i was needing,
what my heart and soul felt safe in
or needed to feel safe in.

so i had to cut it off.
the words.
the breath.
the hope in something that wasn't there.
the dream I had dreamt so many nights
over and over again.
the trust.
the love.
the friendship, even,
for i can't go back to just friends
right now.
the friendship wasn't here.
nor was it there.
i needed time.
i needed space.
i needed me without him,
wholly and completely.
i needed myself
by myself
to heal,
to be,
to cry,
to scream.
this night was completely awful.
and it was the anniversary of Kym's death.

this was the last time we talked.
that was the last he heard from me,
those were the last sights of blurry lines
this time, between him and i.

just fly

no questions.
no veils. no hiding.
no living under the expectation of someone else.
just be.
breathe in the truth
and let it out.

i received a text and
couldn't stay silent any longer.
the thoughts weighed on my heart until i typed it all
out
and told them exactly what happened.
Mats and Monica, i had to let them know
about me and Paul.
i didn't want to be included in group texts
with him anymore,
which they had been doing so sweetly,
keeping in touch from where they were
after departing from León
to check in with me and my whereabouts
along the way.
we were a lively foursome,
all together from Roncesvalles to Pamplona.
but not anymore.
they hadn't suspected anything
for i kept everything under tight wraps.
but i couldn't any longer and they understood,
gave their deepest sympathies and love.
even though it hurt like hell,
it was necessary.
it was good,
this letting go.
long overdue.

for one cannot fly while tied to a branch,
even in the highest of trees
or on the longest of strings.

day 37 - Arzúa to O Pedrouzo

tears on a sunny morn

i messaged a friend,
seeking solace and words of encouragement.

read this morning while eating breakfast
through teary-eyes and a hurting heart
on a hill outside of a stand-alone café,
under an umbrella
looking out at green fields and a road up ahead,
my long road for today...

"Sabrie,

You are on a literal and rhetorical
journey that I don't fully understand...
You've faced some pretty shitty personal
challenges...

As I look at your pictures, especially the
fog-filled stretches, I couldn't help but
think about the girl I knew. The girl who
was shy until she was ready not to be.
You followed your heart, even when your
head told you otherwise. You marched to
a beat that was all your own and didn't just
follow the crowd.

I say all of this to remind you that even
though we live life and it shapes our view
of the world, it doesn't change who we are
at the core.

You're not only likable, you're lovable. It's
ok for you to want some space and be the

same person who wants to curl up in a lap
like a cat."

these words,
i needed.
these words
had golden glue plastered
all over them.

a shared journey

through texts,
emails,
social media,
and phone calls,
I've shared my journey
with friends all over the world.
in spirit
online
and in real time.

people don't have to be in your physical presence,
or even in your closest circle,
to be of support.
energy (spirit) is real
and i feel it all over me.
i've felt it throughout my time here
across this magnificent landscape and portal,
and i know i'll continue to feel it
throughout my turn-around
and
return home.
i know i am not alone.

this,
i do know so far.

i'm going to miss

i'm going to miss my walks with the cows...
how they come up and smell my pack
to make sure
i'm okay
or perhaps to look for something to eat.
but at this point, both are totally fine by me.

i'm going to miss my walks with the birds...
how they wake and sing beautiful songs
to ease this heart to its feet,
to start a new day as always -
everything will be okay.

i'm going to miss the random visits from dogs...
their gentleness in needing a pet or a pat,
a little love from a stranger,
or perhaps not a stranger at all.

i'm going to miss the strength of the horses
grazing in the fields alongside the Way...
how they look up to see who's walking by
then return to their grazing in trust that
i'm okay.

i'm going to miss
so much
of this Way
and all that's walked alongside me
as i've dried my tears and created space for
love and laughter,
as i've said my goodbyes
and hellos
for ever and after.

journal entry: May 9, 2022

With one more day until Santiago,
you'd think all of my tears would've fallen by now,

but...
i cried so much on the trail today.
i even cried to my roommates in my albergue,
people I'd never met before but trusted
in ways
i've never trusted others before.
Maybe it's because i'll probably never see them again,
this close to the end, there's not a lot of time
to really get to know someone.
So i cried. i just cried.
They witnessed some of the strongest emotions from me
today
and were totally okay with it.

Letting go
and beginning again -
one of the hardest things to do.

You can appreciate,
or understand with logic,
a separation
and still
be saddened by it.

But
as odd as it is to say,
i do feel lighter,
i do feel fuller,
i do feel i can walk
into Santiago now
clean,
unburdened,
untroubled
with open lungs and a fresh heart.
And once i reach Santiago de Compostela,

perhaps my real Camino begins.
Taking home
everything i've experienced here,
everything i've learned about myself
and those around me
and bring it to life in my
daily work, love, and play
back in the States.
The strength. The resilience. The love. The community.
It's all here for the taking
and the keeping
and the sharing
and the giving.

As you come full circle, you know
it was all
a part of the process.

knowing goodbye

when she laughs instead of cries
when she dances instead of cradles
when she smiles just because...
you're a memory to her,
you are
what was.
(goodbye)

day 38 - O Pedrouzo to Santiago de Compostela

journal entry - May 10, 2022 (6:00 am)

Last day of my walk to Santiago.

800km/500mi from St. Jean Pied de Port
in the south of France
and across Spain, east to west,
Sunday, April 3 to now.
On average, my daily walks, or hikes
(because let's be honest... much of it WAS hiking over, across,
or down some tough terrain)
consisted of 18-25km (12-16mi).

It's hard to remember the beginning.
It's hard to remember yesterday.
And yet, my memory feels so vividly full.

Each town, big or small, had their own quirky and unique
intricacies, energies, and tastes.
And for the most part, i cannot tell you their names.
So much has passed by,
Or rather, in a more honest statement,
i've walked through so much.
If i sit and reminisce over journal entries and photos, i can
tell you exactly what i was doing at any moment in time.

However,
sitting here in the last early morning café on my Camino...
drinking my last early morning café con leche and
eating my last early morning napolitana de chocolate,
i couldn't speak a solid, meaningful sentence if i tried.
But i am new.
i am changed.
i am full.
For my eyes have seen the world through a different light.
And i can feel it.
Something has taken over and is seated in my soul.

But to place a finger on it now,
to name it,
to say it out loud,
i cannot yet do.

There is one thing i can do though...
On this last day of walking to Santiago, i can tell you now
that what i am feeling is this -

Perhaps my true Camino begins
today in Santiago de Compostela.
Perhaps my true Camino begins
where all of this Way ends...

journal entry - May 10, 2022 (10:30pm)

i'm here.
i made it
to Santiago.
Around 12:30-1pm.
It was amazing.
Walking in, there was a man playing bagpipes for
all the pilgrims coming in.
i wondered if everyone else thought he was playing
just for them too...
walking underneath the arch and into
the plaza,
i nearly collapsed right there.
Overwhelmed.
Happy.
Sad.
Accomplished.
Strong.
Loved.
Supported.
But also a touch lonely
if i'm being honest.

i walked further into the square, to the front of the Cathedral
and stood,
stared in awe.
Turning in a   s l o w   circle
looking at all the people around me,
pack still on my back, a couple stopped me
to congratulate me.
i knew i had seen them before
somewhere along the Way
but i couldn't place where...
She said,
"I know we met somewhere, I just can't remember where!"
i agreed and smiled and said, "i know, me too!"
It's hard to remember exactly where you were when certain
things happened or who you were with, because everything

seemed to melt into a beautiful kaleidoscope on this day so
far from the start.
She gave me a big hug and offered to take my photo.
i turned around to have the Cathedral at my back and
then i placed the time and space of our meeting!
They were the dad and daughter team i met in Villafranca
while having a coffee and tortilla next to the Medieval
castle, being called Pippi by the locals!
At this point, they were already off,
suitcases trailing behind in hand,
into the growing crowd of visitors in the square,
ready for their train out of Santiago and on their way home.

i then saw Erik from Denmark,
he said he was hoping he'd see me walk in.
He asked for the title of my book and said,
"I'm going to keep my eye out for it."

Oh, the friends i've made.

i took it all in...
sat down
and started crying.
Exhausted.
Hungry.
Happy.
Loved.
Embraced by Spirit
and recognized by so many faces around me.
Proud of myself,
oh so proud.
i did it!
Five. Hundred. Miles. All on my own.
if i can do this, i can do anything.

Tears continued to fall
without hesitation or an end in sight,
sitting there,
face in hands
sun on my back
backpack at my feet

in the middle of the Cathedral Plaza.
i felt seen.
i felt heard.
but i still couldn't help it.
Tears raced down my face
like a dam that had just been unsealed.
And i let them
right there in the middle of the square.
Crying my soul out
and back in
to me.
It felt good.
It felt cleansing.

i don't know how long i sat there crying,
for it's what i needed to do
until i had no more tears to give.
And only when they had had all of their space to say,
i stood up and walked around a bit,
wiping the tears away
slinging my pack onto my back
again...
and i saw Choi!
Sweet Choi.
She walked me to the Pilgrim Office,
explained what i needed to do to get my Compostela
and waited for me.
She had plans with a friend for later in the afternoon
but she wanted to make sure i got everything i
needed/wanted.
We gave each other hugs goodbye and said,
"til we see each other again."

Then i saw Gary from Australia
and a few others i couldn't remember the names of.
Just faces,
but simultaneously recognizing each other,
giving warm smiles
and big Congrats!

i checked into my airbnb,

changed,
rested a bit,
then met up with Suzanne for a little light shopping
and dinner.

i'm exhausted now though.

i didn't sleep well last night.
i got up at 5am and was out the door by 6.
Everyone else was up too,

it felt like there was a force drawing us out of bed and
onto the road to Santiago.

It feels amazing to be here though.
Surreal, so much has happened.
i've walked through so much since April 3rd,
it's hard to remember it all.
One day i'll sift through the papers, the receipts,
the photos, the journal entries
and remember.
But for now,
sleep,
i'm so tired.

'Til tomorrow.

santiago de compostela

"It was only a sunny smile, and little it cost in the giving, but like morning light it scattered the night and made the day worth living."

- F. Scott Fitzgerald

midnight in the cathedral plaza

i met up with Stephanie, from Germany,
the girl i met with Mats and Monica
next to the duck pond...
we went for drinks and a bite at
a Taberna do Bispo - a must-visit
per my good friend and fellow peregrino Chardmo.
oh the tapas!
muy delicioso... no need to go anywhere else for dinner,
this.
is it.
we sat at the bar -
she speaks better Spanish than i do,
so she did most of the ordering.
i just pointed and said, "¡Si!"
we chatted for a long time over wine
and the most delicious food in Spain.

we then headed towards the Cathedral
to hear the famous Spanish band that plays there
every night
in the main square.
every night
for pilgrims.
the energy was bubbling
and infectious.
the open plaza was empty and dark
while everyone crowded around the band
underneath the roof of the building facing
the Cathedral.
nothing but the moonlight shining through
a cloudless sky.
as the beautiful Spanish music played,
we laid down on our backs
right there in the middle of the plaza
and looked up.
"you just have to see the cathedral upside-down,"
she said with fervor.
i felt like a kid in midsummer seeking knowledge

amongst the stars.
clouds had filled the sky for the majority of the day
but now
they had parted and left for the evening,
bringing us a sparkly night by which to admire
this greatness.

**just the moon and its stars and these gorgeous
Cathedral spires...
while the band played Viva España into a peace i've
only dreamt of and desired.**

one door, one hall

one door, one hall,
we reminisced through it all.

your face no longer blue,
you were a force to get me through

my divorce, so recent
you gave advice, most decent.

but I fell quick and hard
for your presence and charm.

your smile lit me up
this night, was enough.

you said, "this way,"
and excitement filled my face.

my nerves, you made calm
with wine and an understanding balm.

you knew, with the sweetest grin,
how to let me right in.

we talked and laughed
of our delicate pasts.

i cried until you
showed me your truths.

i sat, and you cleaned
the dishes, and i beamed

at pictures of your kids,
your book, and when

you showed to me
your wedding story.

she was in white,
your beautiful wife,

until when she broke
the vows you both wrote.

the words you framed
still hang acclaimed.

i thought how sweet,
you are one to keep.

we sat and you played
jazz and i stayed.

you brushed my lips
with warm fingertips.

your breath on my neck
for a while, for a sec

was just enough
for me to feel loved.

your skin on mine
was so divine.

but when that day came
you claimed it's too late,

i broke, i was mad
at the world just like that.

one door, one hall,
i walked through it all.

no you, no us,
no more casual touch.

no wine, no glass.

martinis in the past.

that face, those eyes,
that mouth bearded nice,

so soft to touch
but no more to love.

i wish you well.
my dear, your spell

held me so close,
in dreams we spoke.

to be just friends
is strange though i pretend

to be okay
even to this day.

you gave to me
one thing to believe...

myself in this world
around me, everything unfurled

a door, for you Paul -
thank you, after all.

journal entry - May 12, 2022

Tonight is my last night here
in Santiago.
i went to mass and cried a bit.
Grateful for the lingering mask requirements,
for it was easy to hide the tears,
though my red, puffy eyes told a different story.
Such a bittersweet feeling.
Leaving.

i've found comfort in these streets,
these plazas
that great spiritual cathedral rising
to the clouds and back.
But mostly, i've found comfort in the Camino and
it holding my hands and feet through
intense emotions and feelings,
holding space for me to unfold
into this openness
so new
to me.

It's sad to be leaving,
though all of my friends are now gone
off to wherever their lives are leading them now.
i wonder where mine is leading me to...
This,
i don't know quite yet.

i do know i'm off to Bilboa for three nights,
then to Vernon-Giverny for two
(a visit to Monet's Gardens is a must),
then back to Paris for two,
then home.

It's almost time to take my Camino back
to the real world.

But not yet, and for that
i am glad.

trust and unwrap

enjoy the journey.
take each step with intention,
feel the earth beneath your feet.
take as many photos of the poppies
beginning to bloom.
talk with as many horses and cows along the Way
as you choose.
sit with the birds and learn their songs.
feel the wind as it washes through you,
sinking into the depths of your lungs,
embracing your hurt and wrapping it into a tight ball
to disappear and dissolve,
(re)making you whole.
take the direction that speaks to your soul.
recognize others along the Way,
though strangers at first,
your journeys similarly replay
tied together with a beautiful golden string,
your bonds, invisible.
held, loved, and reassured
you're okay,
you are enough.
you're on the right path.
and in this, my dear,
you've come to trust and unwrap.

my finisterre

"The world breaks everyone and afterward, many are strong at the broken places."

- Ernest Hemingway

journal entry: May 14, 2022

I woke early
here in Bilboa
in time to take an early bus to San Pelaio.
From there I walked,
hiked
almost 4 miles to San Juan de Gaztelugatxe,
one of the places used for filming Game of Thrones'
Dragonstone.
Of course, Dragonstone was CGI'd into the shots
but those hundreds of stone stairs,
immense
intimidating
and ancient,
weaving higher and higher
amongst sea and sand,
wind and waves,
the sun and the sky,
are as real as my heart beating and breathing
faster and faster,
anxious to get to the top.

Atop
sits a tiny chapel built in the 9th century
by the Knights Templar for St. John the Baptist.
Though it's been (re)built over the years due to
fire and destruction,
it still holds legend and history,
energy and spirit.

And this Spirit...
I knew,
for I was always going to end up here.
Somehow,
someway...
for it was (unbeknownst to me at the time)
the photo I pulled off the internet to accompany my playlist
for my Camino training

all those months back when I was
planning and prepping.

The Camino knows.
Spirit knows.
It calls when you're ready
and helps when you're here.

This view,
this endless ocean ahead
reaching high
into the sky
so blue
so fine.

Gaztelugatxe, my Finisterre.

she (from the inside)

i no longer mourn you, Jude.
i mourn not having someone there
at the end of the day,
the absence of a goodnight kiss,
the death of a future
i thought was so sure,
the thought of growing old together...
but i no longer mourn you anymore
because what we had
was a sand castle that got ripped away with the tides.
the time we spent apart
only hid the sides of us that were
too jagged and rough, too much to ever
fit into the puzzle we so desperately tried to (re)create.

i no longer mourn you,
but perhaps i mourn the person i was
when i was with you.
she could've used my help
but i left her to fend for herself.
she was enough but
she was different.
and that different didn't fit
your different.
that different didn't fit
your view on things
or how you wanted them to be.

she was wild
but she held it in
for you.

she was emotional
but she quieted it all
for you.

she was spirited
but she blew out her flame

for you.

your leaving broke her
but it freed the spirit inside.
your silence tore through her
but it carved the strength inside.
she is who she's meant to be,
is (re)becoming that girl
she was born to be.
it just took your leaving
your silence
your absence
to break her open and free her
from the inside.

unloved you

she unloved you
as hard as this earth beneath her feet.
she unloved you
as slowly as the towns approached through the cold
and the heat.
she unloved you
with every piece of her soul that held you tight.
she unloved you
in every dream she dreamt in the night.
she unloved you
through valleys and streams
and the hopes she unweaved.
she unloved you
through so much pain, she thought she'd melt into wax
never to be whole again.

but she knows now
she unloved you for the best of things,
for something new.
she knows now you weren't meant to be,
and because of your leaving
she knows her truth.

through the road back home

dusty dusty roads
covered boots in mud and pain
looking out for a town, again
with eyes so weary from the Way
like the burdens that we play
over and over for those to hear,
new friends that become so dear
in days that seem to have no start or end,

now i understand

why i came to walk all this way
all the memories i would repeatedly play
in hopes of letting go some day.
i was so naive
i did not know how,
perhaps i'll let go now.

sweet and sensitive souls
those who suffer in silence still
make their way to these enchanted hills
with hope and longing in their broken hearts,
stories open to depart.
spritely steps in sodden hues
a path treaded by the lucky few
will transform you in ways you'd've never known,

now i think i'll grow

into the person i need to be
you may say it's quite selfish of me
but i'll fight to be free
of these chains and judgements that are laid
for far too many days at my feet.
for i could not love me
until you forced me yet to see
all those times i gave myself
over to something, someone else

i gave it all, it wasn't ever meant to be
but now i know why it has ended -
this world is better off without a Jude and me.

ever-knowing road,
poppies smile in endless fields
wisty vines climb high to heal
the days that run long and hard and slow
like the storms that perfectly know
how to jolt the strong and well-laid plans
uncertainty calls to awaken these hands
who write these words and can't forget,

in me, i will forever bet.

so now i will love me
and all that's on the verge of happening
for life is good and comforting,
i'm okay with being me.
it doesn't matter what other people think,
what matters is this in my heart
and all i've been placed here to be...

goodbye to the girl

goodbye to the girl
you thought you knew,
she was only a facade
she was not true
to herself, or to you
just some image to value.
a made-up version
of your perfect dream,
a fantasy fairytale
that cracked at the seams.
a fancy, celebratory balloon
that was meant to be popped
and shattered into a million pieces
impossible to glue together, she once thought.

but now she knows she was always the glue,
that gold she needed to find was her,
not her union with you,
the one you so easily unwound
yet still she stands ever true.
yes, here she stands
in glitter on the floor
with mud on her shoes
and hope forever more.
shining brightly for all to see,
in front of you, in front of me,

unafraid of her nights anymore
...she gracefully walks through the door.

and now my Camino begins

i walked the 800 kilometers/500 miles
through Spain,
the ancient trail of the Camino.
i shed more tears
than kilometers along the Way.
i'm sure i looked exhausted and sad
in every way possible.
maybe that's why the French man took pity on me.
he explained the taxis sitting across the street...
explained red means unavailable
and green, available.
i had made it back to Paris, though, just barely,
but missed my train to Giverny
where my Airbnb was booked.
it was either buy an expensive
last minute room in a Paris hotel
or make my way, somehow, to Giverny
and not forfeit my charming Airbnb with Martine.
thankfully the French are not
what we Americans make them out to be,
for they were very helpful
in directions given to me,
even the taxi driver who elected to drive
an hour and a half to my destination from Paris -
regardless of being late for dinner at home
and upsetting his partner.
yet another example of
Angels on the Camino
showing up along the Way
when i needed their wings to fly
a little bit further
or find my place to stay.

and now my Camino begins again
ever so gratefully
on this day.

"Learn to trust the journey
even if you do not understand it.
Sometimes what you never wanted or expected
turns out to be exactly what you needed."

- unknown

epilogue

i'm sorry the world
made you feel insignificant and small
that even the dust particles on your desk
seemed ten-thousand feet tall.

i'm sorry the world
ripped your heart out from within
and made you feel it would never
fit back in again.

i'm sorry the world
took the people you loved,
leaving you with not a damn thing to do about it
but wish you were in the clouds above.

i'm sorry the world
took your dreams with the tide
and swallowed you up whole
within the ocean herself, inside.

but the world is a good place, my dear,
for this i know in my heart...
the world is good and kind and new
and you and i are never too far apart.

as you sit by the ocean,
as her horizons hold you near,
you'll see within those endless waves
there is nothing here to fear.

in those clouds above,
in those sunsets so fragrant, i believe
lie the secrets to all of this in the world,
just watch, you wait and see.

you'll thread your pieces back together
with a needle in the darkest of nights.
you'll heal your hurting heart and soul

and keep your head held high.

so place that one foot in front of the other
and you'll reach your Santiago.
in you, you'll find strength to move forward -
in this, my friend, i so very well know.

gratitudes

to the beautiful souls i now call friends, these fellow pilgrims who became "home" as i walked miles and miles across Spain, these kindred spirits who showed as much vulnerability as the land we walked across, who graciously carved spaces within my heart for a love greater than i ever imagined:

Mats and Monica Magnusson, you can't even begin to know how much you mean to me. the head of my Camino family, you both grew to be. thank you for taking me under your wings, for the ropes on how to use trekking poles, for the shoulders to lean on, for the care and concern and checking-in when we were in different villages and even in different parts of the world after our physical Camino ended. forever and always, your american friend. skål!

Jacinda (Jacey) Gedney, your vibrancy kept me going in moments i needed it most. i'll always remember the chocolate you gave me when i arrived in Atapuerca. "you look like you need this," you said. and i did. you just knew. the laughter, the tears, the sisterhood, the boosts of confidence, i'm grateful for it all. thank you so much, friend. so much love.

Stephanie Becker, thank you for all your enthusiasm and inspiration along the Way. we became fast friends from trying to find somewhere to eat in Melide during a siesta and devouring fresh churros from the street market, to dinner and bar hopping in Santiago and gazing at the stars in an empty plaza beneath the Catedral de Santiago de Compostela. we talked as if we'd been friends for years... a true friendship i've found in you. may we see each other again soon.

Werner Alvestad, you quite literally took me under your wing, teaching me all about the birds of the Camino and providing a safe space to talk along

the Way. thank you for your guidance and steady
communications, even from a far. a dear friend, i
consider you to be. one day i'll make it to Scandinavia
and we'll forage for mushrooms!

Heayoung Choi, you were a delight to walk with. happy
and inspirational. thank you for your endless smiles
and generous spirit.

Kerstin Kofer, a gentle soul even birds enjoyed eating
breakfast with. thank you for your sweet friendship
and quiet guidance along the Way.

Bekah Davis, you were always a bright light, finding
the good in any situation. thank you for your
generosity, kindness, and inspiration... and for your
Spanish when the rest of us were stumbling!

Marianne O'Brien, we had many soulful conversations.
i appreciate the space to open up and your words of
encouragement. always wishing you well, my friend.

Martin Dahl
Emily Sauerzapf
Gary
Moritz
Helma
Erik
and the rest of the pilgrim community...
all the airbnb hosts, hospitaleros, volunteers, and shop
keepers along the Way who woke before the morning
sun or opened their doors before time permitted to
make coffee, to make sure we were comfortable and
taken care of, and to make certain we were warm
enough in our beds with extra blankets and logs in the
furnace.

thank you. from the depths of my soul.

- - -

and to those not physically on the Camino but who supported from afar:

Anna Lovind, for showing me i could give time to my creative life and write a book inside and around the moments of chaos that inevitably fill our lives in one way or another. i continue to be inspired by you, hanging quotes of yours above my desk, little reminders that i **can** do this. i thank you, my friend.

Mai Segurel, thank you for showing us around Paris. we had the best time seeing all the sights we were able to see by foot in such a short amount of time. i will never forget it. one day i'll be back in Paris and hope to see you and grab coffee again. love, life, compassion, and elephants <3

Janice Wiehahn (Pittaway), you became a true friend through the realms and a guiding star towards Alexander John Shaia's book, *Returning From Camino*. i can't thank you enough for the support and inspiration and encouragement to share as many photos as i wanted to:) one day we'll go back and volunteer on the Camino together! ¡un café con leche por favor!

Paula Amiss and Joaquin Gonzalez, for being two of the best friends i never thought i'd make and for meeting me *in person* in Bercianos del Real Camino on one of the hardest days along my Way. this universe works in mysterious and beautiful ways. i know i'll always have a "home" in you and Madrid. lots of love xo

my mom, Ashley King, for your unwavering support and love and for watching over my kids while i was gone.

my kids, Addison, Elizabeth, and Finn, for holding down the fort and picking each other up (physically and emotionally) when i couldn't be there to do it.

my brother, Patrick King, for answering my midnight calls and being a solid place to stand in moments of doubt and quicksand. for the inspiration, guidance, and laughter too... you hold Dad's sense of humor so close to your heart and i love it. never let it go.

Steve Bishara, for reminding me who the hell i was in moments i needed it most. your words came through the mist and the fog as clear as the night sky in Santiago de Compostela. i am forever grateful for our friendship and (re)connection. you will always have a special place in my heart.

Gabriel Baez, for introducing me to Rupi Kaur and her beautiful poetry.

Scott Palombo, for your friendship, motivation, and impressive enthusiasm.

Kim Narenkivicius, owner/keeper of The Stone Boat in Rabanal del Camino, for my enchanted stay in your sweet cottage, for the delicious zucchini bread, warm tea and Jameson, for your endearing welcome into your town after a very rainy walk in, and for your advice and inspiration upon writing this book. bringing these pages to life at The Stone Boat was a magical experience. a week of my life i will hold close to my heart, as close as i hold our friendship. forever and always.

my beta-readers and dearest friends: Jacey Gedney, Kelly McGavic Dunne, Allison Tekin, Adrienne Mayo, and Steve Bishara.

to my amazing editor, Cara Trent of Midnight Quill... i am without words. your impeccable attention to detail and guidance when my words were lacking... your time and dedication in helping me make this book the best it could be... your care and encouragement through the long days and many discussions... all of that and more is appreciated beyond worlds. thank you, thank you, thank you. ready for the next one?!

Dave McCann, for being a sounding board, a safe place for endless inquiries, and a heart full of encouragements. without you, getting this book to print would've been a much more tedious and expensive adventure. you helped me believe i could do a lot of it on my own, and for that i am forever grateful. but perhaps i'm most grateful for the friendship and connection we've found along the way. a comfort through it all.

And last but certainly not least... Richard Woodruff, aka Chardmo, my initial influence, my *OG Inspo*, for walking the Camino. thank you for the phone calls and advice, the emails and the texts, from whether i should take a sleeping bag and/or sleeping mat to how to get over a broken heart and move beyond the pain i was plunging through. you've been a true friend through this journey and a witness unlike any other. forever grateful and sending so much love from the bottom of my heart.

Buen Camino <3

about the author

Sabrie King is a writer living in Jacksonville, Florida. At the age of 5, she sat at her small wooden desk, having just played "school" with her sister, practicing letter shapes and handwriting skills on practice sheets galore... telling herself, "this [writing] is what you're meant to do." Now 42 years later, she's made her dream come true. With mud on her shoes and hope in her heart, she writes about her travels and inspirations through the world around her - sharing the magic that many of us lose while journeying from childhood to adulthood. When not writing from her desk or wandering cities and countrysides, you can find Sabrie serving patrons in Historic Avondale at the Biscottis Restaurant.

sabrieking.com
email: sabrieking@gmail.com
instagram: @sabrieking_

"The earth has music for those who listen."
– William Shakespeare

i am ready...

to jump in your fires
to swim in your seas
to soar through your skies
to walk this land you keep

www.ingramcontent.com/pod-product-compliance
Lightning Source LLC
Chambersburg PA
CBHW031443160726
47994CB00005B/1847